RISE
ABOVE
CHAOS

RISE
ABOVE
CHAOS

THE **FIVE PRINCIPLES** TO DISCOVER
SIGNIFICANCE AND **LIVE IN PEACE**

ERICK RHEAM

TEAM
RHEAM
PUBLISHING

RISE ABOVE CHAOS

The Five Principles to Discover Significance and Live in Peace

ISBN   978-1-5445-2819-9   *Hardcover*

978-1-5445-2820-5   *Paperback*

978-1-5445-2821-2   *Ebook*

CONTENTS

INTRODUCTION

"I KNOW WHAT YOU WANT ME TO SAY, BUT I'M NOT GOING TO SAY IT."

Words I didn't expect from my mother. My heart sank as I fought back the lump forming in my throat. It wasn't what I wanted to hear, but it was what I needed to hear. Wise advice from a woman who saw a bigger picture. She fought her motherly instincts to comfort me and instead challenged me.

Life is made up of a series of pivotal moments. This was one of them for me. As a new cadet at the United States Military Academy at West Point in New York, I wasn't prepared for what the academy demanded of me. A recruited high school cross-country and track star, I chose to compete at West Point—an iconic institution with its roots dating back to the American Revolution.

I entered as a runner but soon realized that this place was much bigger than that.

A few short months before that life-altering phone call to my mother, I was a senior in high school with an above-average GPA, but I was fast enough as a runner to garner attention from several NCAA programs.

Two schools stuck out for me: the United States Military Academy and the United States Naval Academy. For me, it boiled down to army or navy. Both had strong running programs. In the end, I chose West Point and started that summer, excited to begin my college career as a runner.

I freely entered the gates at West Point in the summer of 1991, but soon, I felt trapped.

Life at West Point, especially for a new cadet, is chaotic. Upperclassmen yelled and screamed at every turn. Nothing I did was right. I got little sleep. I was hungry, frustrated, and homesick. I was thrown into the military life, and I wasn't sure it was for me.

One damp and cold morning during a very early and very long forced-road march, I stared off into the darkness, alone in my thoughts. I questioned my intentions for coming here. Had I made a mistake?

Of course, I concluded. *Why am I here? I'm a runner, not an army officer. I can run and compete anywhere.*

Most of my high school friends enrolled at Indiana University back home. I was sure I could contact the head coach at Indiana and transfer there.

By the time that road march was over, I had made up my mind. I was coming home.

But my mom had other plans.

"I know what you want me to say. I'm not going to say it. I'm not going to give you permission to come home."

At first, I was angry. Then I was distraught. Didn't she understand what I was going through in that moment? Surely, my mother, of all people, would want what was best for me. I fought the tears and listened to her explanation.

"Give it a year. That's not a long time. See how it goes. And if you still feel the same way, then you can come home."

"There's no way I can stay here for a year, Mom!" I couldn't fight back the tears any longer.

"I know it feels like that right now, but here's what will happen. You will adapt, but more importantly, you will make friendships and build lifelong relationships. If you quit now, you'll regret it. Give it time and see how it goes."

I reluctantly agreed.

We never had that conversation again because she was right. I did adapt and formed lifelong relationships. That conversation changed my life and set into motion a series of events that influenced the life I have now.

From that day forward, I lived out the story I thought I needed to live.

I did everything I thought was right when I began my adult life. I graduated from West Point, started my career, found the young woman I would marry, and started a family. I was on the right path, or so I thought.

Then I hit a brick wall. I never saw it coming. In fact, it was more than just a brick wall. It was rock bottom, and it came in the form of three nearly simultaneous gut punches.

Gut Punch One

"I deserve better than this."

My young wife, Alia, stared at me, her eyes bloodshot from crying. It tugged at my soul because they revealed her disappointment. She was the woman of my dreams—my best friend. She'd chosen me and I'd chosen her, yet I'd failed her. She wanted, deserved, and demanded more.

Up to that point in our young marriage, I'd rejected her. In fact, I'd rejected my newborn daughter, Ashley, too. It wasn't that I didn't love them. I just failed to engage with them. I became distant and unresponsive, and I had no motivation to develop meaningful relationships with them. Alia would have none of it, so she challenged me that day.

Gut Punch Two

"Get out!"

Those were the words that I screamed as I physically pushed my father out of my house. My twin sons, Ryan and Adrian, were newborns, and my parents had flown out to be with us. They wanted to see their new grandchildren, spend time with us, and help us get adjusted to our new arrivals.

They planned to stay ten days, but Dad lasted only two. We got into an argument, and I flew into a fit of rage. Have you ever had that out-of-body experience when you get mad and do things you know are wrong, but you can't stop yourself? That's how I felt. My dad went home that day, and we didn't speak for six months.

Gut Punch Three

"You're suspended."

The human resources manager with the city of Loveland, my employer, searched my eyes for a reaction as he notified me that I would be suspended for a week without pay.

That was my punishment after a weeklong investigation into allegations that I had abused my power as the key accounts manager for Loveland Water and Power. I lacked empathy for others. I lacked situational awareness. And I was angry. I was a rudderless ship in a sea of chaos with no idea on how to get back on track.

It was 2005. I was thirty-two years old, and I was totally lost.

I had no answers because I didn't even know the questions I needed to ask. All I knew in that moment was that I had failed in three major areas of my life. I'd failed as a husband and father. I'd failed as a son. And I had failed at my career.

Something needed to change.

I awoke on Monday morning, the first day of my weeklong suspension, and decided to take a drive to clear my head. I found myself in a small coffee shop in Niwot, Colorado, a quaint little town about forty minutes from my home and fifteen miles north of Boulder. It was close enough so I could get home quickly but far enough that I could escape and reflect on my life and situation.

I spent every subsequent day of my suspension in that little coffee shop in Niwot. I showed up each morning, grabbed a coffee, and sat at a small table next to a window that over-looked the small downtown area. It was quiet but had enough white noise from the baristas working behind the counter that it allowed me to think. I wasn't sure what to do, so I began to write. I started to write a story that turned into a 539-page odyssey of a young man who lost his way and struggled to get his life back on track.

It was an odd way for me to wrap my head around my situation, but it became a vehicle that allowed me to process my life. That week, I mourned, reflected, and searched for answers.

I was frustrated, angry, and bored. But why?

My writing project helped me realize that I lacked purpose and meaning. I had energy but no focus to do anything with it. A person with energy and no purpose is dangerous.

I dug a little further and searched for a word to describe my anger. What was I missing? What was the puzzle piece that would allow me to see the bigger picture?

The word was "significance."

I also searched for a word that described what kept me from significance—that force that fed on my fears, anger, and boredom. I gave it a name.

I called it the Beast. It's an unknown force that can't be seen or heard but felt.

We all have a primary fear. Mine is lack of relevance. It's important that my life is relevant, and back then, the Beast fed off that fear.

I focused too much on what I would become and who I would become. I tried too hard to model myself after other people I admired, like my parents, my successful friends, or other couples. I became lost in the lives and dreams of others. I chased ghosts, and as a result, I lost my identity.

I needed to discover my own form of significance.

I identified the problem: I didn't have a path to my own significance. I'd drifted for too long into a destructive lifestyle, controlled by the Beast. But there was hope. I still had my wife. I still had my family. I still had my career. I'd found my problem, but where should I begin?

This book is about that journey.

It was in that little coffee shop, in that tiny town in Colorado, during that weeklong suspension, at my rock bottom, that my real journey began—a fifteen-year journey of discovery that guided me back to a path of significance.

I realized I wasn't the only one with this problem.

We all desire a life of significance, yet we struggle to find it. We become consumed by our own version of chaos as life races before our eyes, and we slowly lose our grip and drift into obscurity.

I realized that I couldn't keep this to myself. I was not alone. There were thousands of others living in despair, dysfunction, frustration, and anger.

Does this sound like you?

- You've done things right in your life.

- You've hit all the major milestones by getting your degree, starting your career, and starting a family.

- You should be happy, but you're miserable.

- You're frustrated, bored, and angry.

- You're drifting into a destructive lifestyle.

- You're looking for a way out. You want answers but don't know where to begin.

There's good news!

You don't need to take fifteen years to find your own path back to your significance. I want to share with you the five principles that allowed me to cut through the whirlwind of my life, rise above my chaos, and discover my path to significance:

1. **Embrace your spiritual journey.** Build a foundation that is necessary to start and embrace your journey of significance.

2. **Tame the Beast.** Utilize the seven elements of the perfect day to cut through the whirlwinds of your life and tame the Beast.

3. **Leverage the power of encouragement.** Unleash the magic behind encouragement to enhance your most important relationships and attract high achievers.

4. **Ignite your influence and manage change.** Guide the levers of change to ensure your inner circle takes the journey with you.

5. **Master communication and human dynamics.**
    Embrace the art of human dynamics and leverage
    communication skills to form lasting connections.

You have a choice, just like I did in 2005.

You can stick with your current life where you continue to drift
and lose out on valuable opportunities. You can remain bored and
frustrated and drift into a destructive lifestyle. You can continue
to wake up each day exhausted and fearful, with your thoughts
and actions dominated by the Beast.

Or you can choose a life of significance where you live with passion
and purpose. You're emboldened to take steps toward your best
life. You wake up each day energized, excited, and hopeful. Most
importantly, you can learn to make quality decisions to tame
the Beast and ultimately be at peace knowing that you're living a
meaningful life.

I hope you'll join me on this journey and allow me to be your
guide. I'm excited to share with you the beautiful experience of
living a life of significance.

As *New York Times* bestselling author Michael Hyatt said, "The
future, including what's left of today, is a blank canvas. What will
you create?"

If you'd like a quick snapshot of where you are on your significance
journey, along with some action steps to help you move forward,
you can start your journey by taking my free Discover Your Significance Self-Assessment at www.yoursignificanceassessment.com.

Principle 1

EMBRACE YOUR SPIRITUAL JOURNEY

We are not human beings having a spiritual experience.
We are spiritual beings having a human experience.

—Pierre Teilhard de Chardin

For me, 2020 was a very disruptive year. The world shut down because of the global COVID-19 pandemic, and like a lot of people, I found myself stuck at home.

It was fun in the beginning, but it got old quickly.

My family and I searched for ways to fill our days that were once full of purposeful activities like school, work, family dinners at restaurants, movies in theaters, and family trips. That was all gone for now.

Now we hiked, watched movies at home, played games, and cooked. I can't say it was too bad because it gave us an opportunity to slow down and reconnect. There's a lot I will remember from that year, but there was one activity that I especially enjoyed with my family: putting together a puzzle.

It was a silly puzzle of a New York City scene, but it captured my family's attention for almost a week. We laid all 1,500 puzzle pieces on the kitchen table and placed the picture of the scene from the box on the table as a guide.

We took turns contributing to the project. Everyone searched for pieces of the puzzle that fit together, and we found joy in watching the picture slowly take shape in front of us. I became addicted to the satisfaction of when a puzzle piece snapped perfectly into place. I found it hard to stop and lost myself in the activity for hours that spun into days.

There's something deeply satisfying when you discover a missing piece of your life, like a puzzle piece that falls into place. I realized that over the past fifteen years, I've been putting together a jigsaw puzzle that is my life.

Like a jigsaw puzzle, pieces of my life were scattered. It was up to me to find the right pieces that fit together to form my vision for my future—a future that had meaning for me.

Every puzzle must have a beginning, where you find the first piece that fits with another, and thus the journey begins. I believe that starter piece on your journey is encompassed by one singular and profound question:

Why?

There's a spiritual component to humanity. Different religions and societies have different names for it, but we all know it. It's ingrained in our souls. It's that inner voice that constantly asks why.

This is a fundamental question that your soul demands you answer. There is no path to significance without understanding why. Knowing your why is the foundation of your journey. It's your rock that will anchor you during the whirlwinds of life and keep you from drifting into oblivion.

This section will explore your spiritual journey and address why it's important to build a foundation that can withstand attacks from the Beast.

Chapter 1

WHAT DOES ROCK BOTTOM LOOK LIKE?

Rock bottom became the solid foundation on which I rebuilt my life.

—J. K. ROWLING

I LANDED IN TUZLA AIRBASE IN A C130 MILITARY CARGO PLANE with a ton of supplies and another soldier who was on his way to link up with his new unit late one evening in the dead of winter.

It was in the war-torn country of Bosnia-Herzegovina in 1996 that I first encountered the dark side of humanity.

The depth of hatred and vitriol had no limits. The country was no bigger than the state of Alabama, yet it housed over three million undocumented lethal land mines designed to destroy military vehicles and kill soldiers. Unfortunately, those land mines didn't discriminate in what they destroyed. It was not out of the ordinary for children to lose their lives because they accidentally stepped on a land mine.

The people of Bosnia experienced World War II-level genocide. If you were the wrong religion, you were murdered and shoved into an unmarked mass grave. Women, children, elderly, sick, or disabled—it didn't matter. Families were executed and thrown into large pits together.

The world could no longer look the other way; thus, I found myself the newly minted platoon leader of the Second Military Police Platoon, the Wolfpack Platoon, of the 536th Military Police Company, in support of Operation Joint Endeavor. Our mission: stop the Bosnian Serbs and Muslims from killing each other and keep the peace.

I'd never experienced anything like it. The level of destruction was hard for me to grasp. Cities, towns, villages, homes, and entire families were destroyed.

Wiped from the face of the earth.

My platoon conducted missions in once-thriving and -bustling towns that were now reduced to smoldering rubble, with all hope lost.

The human tragedy I witnessed extended beyond the borders of Bosnia and followed me back to my home station in Germany. It was there that I witnessed the struggle of the soldiers desperately trying to reintegrate into society and their families.

I spent several months sifting through the broken lives of the soldiers within my unit. After a year of stress serving in Bosnia and being away from their families, some of them began to abuse their families and hurt one another. That same level of darkness I'd witnessed in Bosnia seemed to follow us back at home.

Did we all possess that level of darkness?

When I laid my hands on my father back in 2005, I felt a level of anger that surprised me. I felt a darkness awaken in me that I recognized because I had encountered it in 1996 while serving in Bosnia and Germany.

The answer was clear.

Not only do we all possess that level of darkness, but I had it living inside of me, and it had the potential to destroy my life. I hit my rock bottom, and I felt the darkness engulf me like a large snake wrapped around my entire body, slowly squeezing all the good out of my life. It was here that I came face to face with the Beast and its thirst for total and utter destruction.

Something had to change.

The fundamental question I asked myself toward the end of my suspension in 2005, in that little coffee shop in Niwot, Colorado, was simple.

Did I have the power and ability to change course and overcome that darkness? More importantly, did I have the power to tame the Beast?

I was determined to answer those questions with a resounding yes.

I ended my week of suspension with clarity on my problem. Now it was time to take my first step out of that pit of darkness and find my way back to a life of significance.

I was in a bad spot in my life; however, I still had my marriage, my family, and my job.

I was hopeful.

It was time to take my first step.

All journeys begin with that first step, but before you can take that first step, you must first acknowledge what you're stepping away from, which in this case is your own version of rock bottom.

Rock bottom is all relative. It doesn't matter how deep your rock bottom is compared to my story or anyone else's. It only matters that you're disconnected from where you are and where you want to be in your life.

Rock bottom comes in many forms. It can be health, family, personal, spiritual, career, or all the above. The Beast feeds off your despair and wants to keep you mired in the emotions you feel when life just isn't working out for you.

It's healthy to acknowledge that you're not doing well and to mourn your losses. I mourned time lost with my father after our fight. I mourned the loss of love and intimacy with my wife. I mourned the loss of respect from my colleagues at work. I took the time to grieve my situation before I gained the courage to act.

What does your rock bottom look like?

First, acknowledge the areas of your life where you're struggling. Write them down in list form, and then meditate on them.

Second, mourn the pain associated with those areas of struggle. Connect the emotions associated with the losses incurred because of your struggles.

Third, acknowledge that you cannot stay here in this rock bottom state of mind. You need to make changes, which is the purpose of this book. I'm going to show you how to gain the courage to make the changes necessary to not only survive your rock bottom experience but to thrive beyond it.

Now it's time to be hopeful, because we're about to take the next step together.

Puzzle piece: Acknowledge your rock bottom. Make a list of things you lost as a result of your rock-bottom experience. Take a moment to mourn those losses. Then commit to take the first step to move away from your rock bottom.

Chapter 2

WHY SHOULD YOU CARE?

The two most important days in your life are the day you are born and the day you find out why.

—MARK TWAIN

WHY?

It's a foundational question we all must answer to survive the darkness and to survive the Beast. Without a why, there is no purpose, and when there is no purpose in your life, the Beast feeds off your pent-up energy and uses it to cause pain and destruction. Without your why, you're doomed to fail and potentially cause pain beyond yourself and to those you love.

Everyone has talent. When a talent is fueled with energy, that talent is like a weapon. It can be used for good or evil. The key is to align that talent and energy with a purpose or a why.

It makes sense but is hard to do because finding your why can be a daunting task. I believe the reason you struggle to find your why is that you get too bogged down with the urgent things in life.

Everything tugs at you and demands your attention now.

It's much easier to take care of the urgent matters of the day than to address a "far-off" future. You always feel like you'll have time to deal with that later, so you put it off for tomorrow, and then the next week, and then the next year. And then a decade passes, and bitterness and regret settle into your heart.

The Beast keeps you busy.

The Beast urges you to solve problems and deal with issues at work and home. It distracts you from what you should really focus on, which is your purpose. Your why.

It's time to stop the cycle and look beyond your daily whirlwind and into your future. Let's start with a simple question that will take you only thirty minutes to answer, but it could be the most important thirty minutes when it comes to your future and your path to significance.

What does a meaningful life look like to you?

Stop what you're doing and pull out a piece of paper. Allow your heart to open up to the possibility of what a meaningful life looks like to you.

Shut the door to your office or go outside on the patio. Head to a coffee shop or your local park. Lock yourself in your car and turn on some music. It doesn't really matter. Just create thirty minutes of space in your life.

You deserve the opportunity to assign meaning to your life.

Something magical happens when you write stuff down, when you get it out of your head and make your thoughts real on a piece of paper. Let's create some magic now, together. Start by asking yourself the question that will jump-start your journey back to significance:

What does a meaningful life look like to you?

Don't be afraid to dream and pour out your soul during this exercise. If you need help getting started, here are some questions to consider:

- What is important to you and why?

- Who is important to you and why?

- What can you not live without?

- How do you want to spend your days?

- Where do you want to spend your days?

After you're done with this exercise, take a deep breath and soak in what you just wrote down on paper. Your soul is speaking to you. You've peered into what could be, which is your version of significance.

Congratulations! You just found your next puzzle piece.

Puzzle piece: Determine your why by writing down what a meaningful life looks like to you. Use the questions listed in this chapter to help you with this exercise.

Chapter 3

THE PROBLEM WITH THE PASSION PARADIGM

Don't ask yourself what the world needs; ask yourself what makes you come alive and do that.

—JOHN ELDREDGE

WHEN I FIRST STEPPED OFF THAT PLANE IN TUZLA AIRBASE in 1996, I was twenty-two years old and nervous about what awaited me on my very first assignment as a platoon leader.

I was more than nervous. I was terrified.

I trained for this moment but felt totally inadequate. How long would it take for my new unit to figure out I was a fraud? Would I be brave enough in the face of danger? Would I make the right decisions?

The Beast cluttered my mind with dozens of these questions and filled me with anxiety.

Luckily, I had a while before the logistical convoy would arrive to take me to my new post. While I waited, I found myself in the chow line at the mess hall. I stood in line behind an older lieutenant colonel who was a few months away from retirement.

The line was long enough that we struck up a conversation. He was kind and generous with his words of encouragement and wisdom. I felt my anxieties begin to fade the more we talked. I think he could sense my trepidation.

"Lieutenant, let me give you a piece of advice that, if you follow it, will serve you well," he said.

My interest piqued. I leaned in to hear his words.

"Don't worry about what the other lieutenants in your unit are doing. Don't worry about what you want to do next in your career either. Just focus on the job you have right now, and be the best at that job you can possibly be," he said as he slid his tray down the chow line and selected his food. "If you follow that simple piece of advice, then success will always be waiting for you."

He nodded and then turned and headed into the mess hall and out of my life.

I pondered his words after that night and tried to live by them.

I believe the passion paradigm we're taught as kids is a lie. You know, the one where you're taught to pursue your passions and chase your dreams.

Total lie.

If you follow that train of thought, you will chase a set of conditions that will never exist, and your passions will always be just out of reach. Here's what it sounds like:

"I will finally finish that degree once my kids get a little older."

"I will pursue that side hustle once things settle down at work."

"Once my boss retires, then I can do the work I love."

Does this sound familiar? It never ends, and it never will unless you shift your passion paradigm.

Your passions are critically important. Stop pushing them off into the future. Leverage them now. Make them part of your life. Allow them to spill into your current situation and become the blessing to your soul and to those around you that they were intended to be.

Carry your passions with you like a backpack. Whatever phase of life you're in right now, unpack your passions and throw yourself into your current situation fueled by your passions. Be the best you can be in that moment.

Unfortunately, I forgot that lesson, and what filled the void was bitterness, which is a tool of the Beast. I needed to rediscover my passions.

For me, it's people.

For whatever reason, people motivate me. Being around others energizes me. Family, friends, acquaintances, or strangers—it doesn't matter. As I dug into this a little further, I realized that my passion isn't just being around people. It's being around inspired people I love.

It thrills my soul to be around inspired people. I wanted more of it; thus, I'd found my passion.

Now let's focus on your passion.

First, you must understand why leveraging your passions is important on your journey to significance.

Life is chaotic and relentless. It's downright hard. You cannot avoid chaos. It's a part of your journey. To live a life of significance, you'll need to learn how to rise above it. That's where your path awaits.

Your passions are the fuel that will elevate you above the chaos.

Without passion, you'll lack the energy to face daily challenges. Your passions are what your soul needs to thrive when the Beast disrupts your days and you feel like retreating to an old disruptive pattern of behavior.

You need your passions. Without them, you'll drift far away from your significance.

What are your passions?

Let's rediscover your passions with four simple questions. Pull out a piece of paper and answer them now.

1. What excites you?

2. What drives you to keep going even when you're tired and frustrated?

3. What do you think about first when you wake up in the morning?

4. What are you willing to suffer for?

Congratulations! By clarifying your passions, you've found your next puzzle piece.

Knowing your passions is critical to significance; however, you need more than just your passion. Living on passion alone won't cut it. It's the fuel to elevate you above the chaos, but you need a vehicle in which to put that fuel.

That vehicle is purpose.

My problem was that my passion for people was getting me in trouble. The more people I engaged with, the more I exposed myself to harm. My passion and energy to relate with others was misguided because I engaged with others without purpose.

An unfettered passion can be dangerous, which is what led to my suspension. Even though I was frustrated and angry, I never lost my passion to engage with others. I was just doing it the wrong way.

I needed a purpose that properly utilized my passions. I will show you how to leverage your passions within a purpose as we continue the journey.

You're doing great. Let's continue this journey together.

Puzzle piece: Uncover your passions by answering the passion questions.

Chapter 4

SUPERPOWERS AREN'T JUST FOR SUPERHEROES

Everybody ends up somewhere in life. A few people end up somewhere on purpose.

—ANDY STANLEY

MY FAVORITE SUPERHERO IS BATMAN.

There are other superheroes with better superpowers and cooler outfits and backstories. They're all cool, but I've always been drawn to Batman.

I think it's because he's just a regular guy. He possesses no super-powers other than money and gadgets.

He's not an alien like Superman. He doesn't possess genetic power like the Hulk. He's not a god like Wonder Woman.

He's just a guy with issues, like me.

Batman is just a human being who discovered his purpose. I can do that; you can do that.

Why are superpowers only for superheroes?

When I was transitioning out of the military into civilian life, I had a mentor, Howie, who was pivotal for me as I struggled to navigate a frustrating time in my life. One of his many lessons was the power of a reading habit. He challenged me to read fifteen minutes a day and to fill my mind with positive information.

Howie's advice started a lifelong habit.

One of the first books I read was *Now Discover Your Strengths* by Marcus Buckingham and Donald O. Clifton. That book gave me permission to shed my weaknesses and focus on my strengths. I'd never thought about focusing my energy on a few key strengths that I possessed. Instead, I spent too much energy on things that I was not good at or that were simply distractions.

I took a strengths-based test that accompanied that book, and it revealed to me that I was a communicator by heart. That planted a seed for future growth within my strengths.

Howie also taught me the power of mentorship and learning from others, which started a habit of listening to positive messages and attending live events.

I discovered an author I connected with in Dr. John Maxwell. I loved his books, but I loved seeing him speak live even more. At one live event I attended, he discussed the idea of rating your skillsets from 1 to 10, with 10 making you an expert at that skill. Dr. Maxwell noted that the best you can do is raise any skillset by two points, no matter how hard you practice or work on that skill.

With that logic, he challenged the audience not to waste their time on skillsets that were between 5 and 7, because the best you can do is raise them to 7 and to 9.

Instead, focus on your natural strengths. Focus on skills where you are an 8 or 9, and turn those into 10+. This was an aha moment for me—a puzzle piece. I turned my attention to my strengths, but I wanted to be more than strong. I wanted a superpower.

I wanted to be Batman.

I discovered three powerful questions that helped me land on my superpower.

What are your friends saying about you?

In the beginning, I pursued speaking opportunities within my career not by design but because I liked public speaking. I did them for free, mainly in breakout sessions at public power utility conferences.

It was at such an event when a friend and former coworker, Dan, approached me after my breakout session and asked me, "When are you going to do this full time?"

"What do you mean?" I responded.

"I mean, you're really good at this. You should speak full time," he answered.

It was a quick conversation but a powerful one.

Many people had mentioned my aptitude for speaking, but he was the first who suggested I pursue it as a career. That triggered something inside me that set off a series of events that led me to where I am now, a full-time professional speaker doing over fifty paid speaking events a year.

What about you?

What are your friends and colleagues saying about you? The people close to you; the ones who are around you the most and know you best, will give you clues to your superpower.

Listen to them and look for patterns.

What things do you do that draw praise? On what topics or issues do people come to you for advice?

What comes easy to you?

For a long time, I just thought everyone liked to speak in a public setting. I didn't give it much thought because it came naturally to me. It wasn't until I began to explore the art and business of speaking that I realized it is a skill that many don't possess or care to pursue.

Public speaking is unique to me.

It's easy for me to identify a hot topic, clarify my thinking on this topic, and translate that thinking into a meaningful message that I can write or speak about in a public setting.

Once I realized that I had a talent for speaking and liked it, I began to explore ways to do more of it.

What are some activities or tasks in your life that you take for granted? These are things that you do without giving them much thought because they are simple for you and you're good at them. Find these things and pursue them more. They could be a path to your superpower.

Where are you getting professional opportunities?

Your natural talents attract opportunities. What are they for you?

Early in my utility career, I was asked to speak publicly on behalf of my employer on many occasions. I didn't think much of it but always welcomed the opportunity. Once I began to think about speaking as a career, I realized that I had been given many opportunities to speak that had prepared me to make the jump.

One afternoon, I got a phone call.

"My name is Russel. I heard you're a public speaker," the voice on the other end said matter-of-factly.

I had never heard anyone call me a public speaker before. I liked it. "Yes. What can I do for you?"

"My friend said you would be a good fit for an event we have coming up in a few months. Are you interested? And how much do you charge?" he inquired.

"Yes, and $1,000 is my fee," I responded. I had no idea how to answer that question. I just came up with the fee with no logic behind it.

"Sounds good! Let's discuss the details," Russel gleefully responded.

It was on that day, with that phone call, that I became a professional speaker, and I've never looked back.

Where are your opportunities coming from, and do you notice any patterns?

There are clues all around you that provide hints about your superpower. Mine them. Meditate on them and lean into them because your superpower awaits you.

Once you land on a superpower and couple it with passion, you've discovered your why. For me, my passion is people. I leveraged that passion with my superpowers of communication and motivation, which led down a path of becoming a public speaker.

Puzzle piece: Discover your superpower by answering the three superpower questions.

Chapter 5

LIVING ON PURPOSE

When you do something, something happens.

—Greg Gilmore

The blazing afternoon sun scorched the sands of Egypt. Jack pulled the reins on the camel he was riding and brought his beast to a complete stop. He turned toward me, sweat dripping off his forehead.

"My contact lens in my right eye just curled up and popped out. Damn, it's hot out here!"

Jack and I were a week removed from graduating from the United States Military Academy at West Point. We decided that we would take a graduation trip together, and we chose Egypt as our destination for two reasons.

First, we had an Egyptian classmate, Ayman, and he agreed to host us once we arrived.

Second, we thought it would be fun.

We found ourselves traversing the hot desert on a couple of camels with a local guide who took us to the pyramids for a personal tour of the ruins.

It was epic!

Jack and I started our adventure the day after graduation, on June 4, 1995. We had a couple of backpacks, our passports, a few thousand dollars of cash between us, and the desire to get to Egypt. That was about it.

We didn't have a concrete plan for how we were going to get there other than we planned to hop on any military logistical flights we could find to get us moving in the right direction.

We started our journey in New York with our first stop in Delaware. There, we waited a few days, trying to find a military flight that had room for us.

Finally, we flew out of Delaware and landed in Georgia.

From Georgia, we flew to the Azores.

From the Azores, we flew to Italy.

From Italy, we hopped on a ship that sailed to Greece.

From Greece, we hopped on a flight to Egypt.

We took buses, planes, trains, boats, taxis, and camels. It was quite the adventure, and it only happened because we weren't afraid to act.

We knew we wanted to get to Egypt. We weren't quite sure how we would get there, so we took the first step, which led us to our next step, and then the next—a series of steps that ultimately got us to our desired destination.

The key to your journey of significance goes beyond just discovering your why. Having the courage to do something about it is when the journey begins.

Having a purpose in life becomes your "true north." When life gets hard and the whirlwind pulls you from every direction, your purpose will guide you back on your path.

The good news with purpose is that there's a formula:

(PASSION+SUPERPOWER)*ACTION = PURPOSE

You've already discovered your passion and uncovered your superpower.

Now it's time to act.

When I completed my first paid gig and cashed my $1,000 check, I was stoked but also frustrated because I wasn't sure what to do next. If I was serious about a speaking career, I needed a plan.

In 2012, I started to follow author and professional speaker Michael Hyatt. I admired his courage to leave his day job and pursue a speaking career. In 2014, I learned that he had partnered with his friend Ken Davis, and they hosted a conference in Florida for aspiring public speakers.

I approached Alia and got her permission to invest money we didn't have so I could travel to Florida and attend Hyatt's conference. It wasn't what I learned at the conference that mattered. What mattered was I took action to explore my passion and superpower.

The act of attending that conference started the flywheel of my speaking career.

I've read several biographies on people I admire: famous political figures, professional athletes, business titans, and social elites. I've personally met and interviewed Super Bowl champions, actors, clergy members, and Hall of Fame basketball players and coaches. And when I finally met my newest hero, Michael Hyatt, in Florida at his conference in 2014, I discovered something that surprised me but also motivated me.

He didn't have all the answers. He was figuring it out, too! He seemed to have some clarity on what he was going to do next, but he didn't have a pristine plan to get him there like I'd expected.

I admired him even more after my trip to Florida because he wasn't afraid to be vulnerable with all of us who attended that conference. It was refreshing.

I discovered that all those successful high achievers I had studied had one thing in common:

They had the courage to act.

They weren't always totally clear on what they were doing; they were just figuring it out along the way. They didn't have a concrete plan for every detail of their lives; they just had a vision and the courage to take the next step. I needed to find that courage.

The problem was the Beast.

The Beast wouldn't go away. It constantly attacked me, especially when I leaned into my purpose. If I was going to be successful, I needed to tame it.

What's the next step you need to take on your journey?

On a piece of paper, write a list of possible actions you could take to move forward in your life. Don't overthink this exercise; just make a list. Then pick the very next thing you can do to move forward and do that. Don't worry about the other steps. Just take the next one, and you will be on your way.

Puzzle piece: Review your list of action items, and identify the one you feel like you can complete next. Don't fret about the overall journey. Just take the next action step on your list.

PRINCIPLE 2

TAME THE BEAST

I've become convinced that every person should treat himself strictly and even rudely and distrustfully; it's difficult to tame the beast in oneself.

—IVAN TURGENEV

THE BEAST IS A MYTHICAL FORCE THAT SHOWS UP IN LITERATURE, movies, and throughout history. It's taken on many names and infinite forms, but one thing is clear: it is real.

The Beast is that force that stands in your way of significance. For whatever reason, it hates a person who lives with purpose. Once you decide to live with purpose and pursue significance, the Beast will revolt and do everything it can to throw you off track.

The only way to fight the Beast is to acknowledge and then tame it. I've discovered a method to tame the primary obstacle you will face as you lean into your purpose, and I'm excited to share it with you.

Get ready for the Beast to show up as you read the next part of this book. It will attempt to distract you and get in your head. It will tell you that what I'm sharing with you won't work.

That's exactly why it will work.

The Beast only gets louder and more aggressive when it's threatened. It will be threatened as your paradigm shifts and the passion of your heart stirs. Be prepared for it to scream in your mind and attack your soul because you're about to lock it in a cage.

Chapter 6

WHAT DOES THE PERFECT DAY LOOK LIKE?

Make every day your masterpiece.

—John Wooden

A PERFECT DAY IS WHEN THE WORLD SEEMS TO BEND FOR YOU. IT starts with a full night of sleep. You fall right asleep when you go to bed and don't wake up until your alarm goes off the next morning.

You wake up rested and ready for the day.

You have a nice hot breakfast; in fact, your eggs are cooked to perfection. Your coffee tastes exceptionally good. It's fresh and hot, and it hits the spot.

You feel energized and ready to start your day.

You have a good hair day. You look in the mirror and like what you see, and when you step on the scale, you noticed you've lost a couple of pounds.

You feel healthy.

You jump in the car with a full tank of gas and head off to work. You're delighted that you get nothing but green lights all the way to work. Your local radio station plays your favorite songs, with no commercials, and you find yourself humming as you pull into work.

The day is off to a great start!

When you walk into work, you discover that your pesky coworker, the one who never has anything nice to say and always seems to find fault in your work, called in sick today.

What a pleasant surprise!

You clear out your emails early in the day, process all your necessary paperwork, and get all your work done on your task list so you can leave work a little early.

That never happens, but you'll take it.

When you arrive home, your spouse greets you with a genuine smile and announces that for dinner, you two should go out and you get to pick the restaurant. You decide to go to your favorite restaurant, and when you arrive, your favorite table is open and your favorite waiter is working. He already knows what you like and brings your beverage of choice and reveals that the special for the night is your favorite dish.

The food, drinks, and atmosphere are pleasant tonight.

You arrive home later that evening, where your normally distant and grumpy teenager decides she wants to have a conversation with you. It's pleasant, and at one point, she hugs you and acknowledges that you're a good parent.

She never does that, and you cherish the moment.

You head to bed early that night with your spouse and binge watch your favorite show on Netflix. Then you turn off the TV and kiss your spouse good night. You take a deep breath and let out a satisfied sigh as your head sinks into your pillow.

Today was a perfect day, you think as you slowly fall asleep.

Where was the Beast today? Did it go on sabbatical or take the day off? No, it was there, but today, it was chained in the corner and not allowed to disrupt your perfect day.

The problem with the perfect day is that it's rare.

It pops up every now and then. Unfortunately, most days are anything but perfect. So how do we experience the perfect day and duplicate it often?

First, let's define the perfect day. To do that, let's discuss what it's not.

It's not a perfect set of circumstances. Your circumstances will always be wrought with challenges and obstacles. Welcome to life on planet Earth.

It's not a set of conditions that must be in place before it can be perfect. If you're waiting for a set of conditions before you truly pursue your passions and do the things you believe you were meant to do, you'll wait forever because those conditions you have set in your mind rarely occur.

It's not about trying to control what you cannot control. When you simply embrace what you can control, you can begin living your significant life.

Once you understand what the perfect day is not, you'll gain the wisdom that the perfect day is not perfect at all. What's perfect is the way you approach your day and respond to what happens to you throughout the day.

So what is the perfect day?

It's about taking deliberate actions to set yourself up for success by surrounding yourself with a layer of protection to guard against the Beast.

It's a mindset—the way you see the world as you approach your day.

If we go back to our perfect day example and dig a little further, we'll discover some nuances that made it perfect.

For instance, you didn't get all green lights on your way to work. On this day, you left home early and gave yourself more than enough time to get to work. You didn't notice the red lights you hit because they didn't matter.

You got your work done today because you were more realistic and intentional with your capacity to get certain things done, and you focused on a few important things rather than overloading your workday with tons of tasks that didn't really matter.

Your teenager was so pleasant with you because you came home with a good attitude, which made the atmosphere such that it was easier for her to sit with you and discuss her day.

The perfect day is more about action and mindset than circumstance. Taking deliberate and proactive action steps allows for the perfect day.

How does this tame the Beast?

I witnessed the destruction of the Beast in Bosnia, in Germany with my soldiers, and within my own life. I was left with two fundamental questions. First, could I get rid of the Beast?

Ask a lifelong smoker who finally quits if he ever craves a cigarette. He'll tell you he does almost every day. In fact, ask anyone who's overcome any sort of addiction if they still struggle with it. The fact is, we're flawed human beings, and the Beast feasts on our flaws.

Second, if I couldn't get rid of the Beast, could I tame it?

That's the good news. We can all tame the Beast with deliberate and consistent action steps.

The Beast feasts on lack of purpose.

When you lack purpose, it leaves a hole in your soul that must be filled. This is a breeding ground for the Beast to birth a purpose for you, and it's usually destructive.

When I lived in Germany, I moved to a small town called Hammerless. On the edge of town was a small bar, and I walked to it on Friday nights to have a few beers. I found myself bellied up to the bar and sharing drinks with soldiers who fought for Nazi Germany during World War II. I engaged in fascinating discussions with these war veterans.

After a few discussions, I finally had the courage to ask my question: how could they fight for a man like Hitler who provoked such hatred and destroyed an entire group of people?

Their response to that question fascinated me.

Those men explained that they never fought for Hitler. They fought for their country and for their families.

Germany as a country was still devasted by World War I when Hitler rose to power. Hitler gave them purpose in the beginning, and they followed him. By the time World War II broke out, it was too late. Germans had to fight for their mere survival.

When a person, an organization, or even an entire country lacks purpose, the Beast fills the void with evil and destruction. Purpose is necessity. The void will be filled with something. Whether it's filled with good or evil is up to you.

Understanding your why by aligning your passions with your superpower and then coupling that with action allows you to live a life on purpose so the Beast cannot distract and destroy.

That sounds easy enough, but it's not.

The problem with the Beast is that it's hungry and it's relentless. The only way to tame it is through a set of daily actions that insulate you from the Beast and allow you the freedom to pursue significance.

I spent well over a decade searching for a set of actions that would free me from the Beast, and I landed on what I affectionally call the seven elements of the perfect day. I learned that when I applied them daily, I was able to cut through the whirlwind of life, rise above my chaos, and find my path to significance. And so will you.

Here are the seven elements of the perfect day that I leverage to tame the Beast:

1. **Manage your priorities.** Focus on the main thing and eliminate the things that distract.

2. **Manage your energy.** Create a healthy life and manage your physical resources.

3. **Work within your strengths.** Eliminate, delegate, and automate areas of weakness.

4. **Live with clarity.** Clarify key components of your life so that you may live purposefully.

5. **Manage expectations.** Create healthy relationships by clarifying others' expectations.

6. **Assemble a team.** Surround yourself with quality people with a common vision.

7. **Build systems.** Craft systems to create the necessary margin to pursue significance.

Take a moment and reflect on how your day went yesterday. How did it go for you? Was it fraught with challenges? How was your attitude at the end of the day? Think about your day and rate it on a scale of 1 to 10. What could you have done differently to make it better?

The shortest path to a more perfect day starts with your attitude.

Make a list of all the challenges you faced yesterday. Next to each challenge, write down what you learned and the opportunity for growth it created for you. This exercise will provide you with a better perspective on your day and your attitude about it.

Puzzle piece: Over the next week, end each day by assessing your attitude about the day. Look for ways to change your attitude by focusing less on the challenges and more on the opportunities those challenges created for you.

I created a companion online course that provides in-depth training on the seven elements of the perfect day. Go to www.theperfectdaycourse.com for more information.

Chapter 7

THERE'S NO SUCH THING AS TIME MANAGEMENT

Perfect Day Element #1: Manage Your Priorities

> *Yesterday is gone. Tomorrow has not yet come. We have only today. Let us begin.*
>
> —MOTHER TERESA

"DO YOU WANT TO BE HERE?"

Those words cut through my heart. Jim, my roommate the second half of my plebe (first) year at West Point, confronted me one afternoon while we were shining our shoes.

Jim was a straight shooter from Ohio. He was a good guy, very smart, and a great roommate. I respected him. I struggled my first year at the academy. I found cadet life to be challenging, and it was difficult for me to balance the rigors of the military, academics, and varsity athletics.

Jim would have none of it, so he stared me in the eyes and challenged me.

"Of course I want to be here!" I responded, offended by his accusation.

"Then something needs to change. You've got to take this stuff more seriously. Let me help you," Jim said. "You have to decide, Rheam. Do you want to be a track star or a cadet? You can't be both!"

Around the same time my roommate confronted me, my track and field coach, Ron Bazil, called me to his office and challenged me as well. I was a recruited athlete for cross-country and track, and I wasn't living up to his expectations.

It was clear the way I approached the daily grind at West Point was not working.

Everything at West Point is ranked: physical, military, and of course, academics. After the first semester, I was ranked in the mid-900s out of 1,100 cadets. I needed to change my approach, but how?

My primary problem was that I didn't know how to study. How I studied in high school didn't work at the academy. I didn't have time to read every homework assignment and study every practice problem.

Luckily, Jim helped me. More importantly, he taught me how to study. I got my grades up, and by the time I graduated from West Point, I'd moved up to the middle of my class.

The trick was to pull out what was most important from the curriculum and focus on that. In essence, I had to prioritize what I would learn and prepare myself for the tests.

West Point presents a series of constraints to force cadets to prioritize. If a cadet cannot learn to prioritize, then he will fail. I didn't thrive at West Point until I learned that lesson.

There's freedom in constraints. It sounds counterintuitive, but it's true.

When's the last time you went on a big vacation? Remember the day before you left? You were super efficient at work to make sure everything was covered. You focused on the most important things because you didn't have time to get it all done. Duplicate your last day before vacation, except with less stress.

My first mistake was that I gave too much power to time. I became obsessed with it. As a result, I never thought I had enough. I always felt like I was falling behind in my race with time.

The Beast used this against me.

It leveraged my warped view of time as a false measurement of my success. I measured everything I did within a construct of time.

Was I progressing within my career on the appropriate timeline?

Was I getting paid enough for my time?

Did I have enough time to spend with my kids?

How much time should it take my kids to learn to walk?

But time is rarely the issue. We all have the same amount of time each day, so how do some seem to get it right while others struggle?

Time passes with or without you. You can't store it, buy it, borrow it, or loan it. It ticks away, methodically, with no regard for your issues.

There's no such thing as a time management problem.

The key is to manage your priorities to make the best use of the time you have.

Biologically, you're not equipped to take on too many big tasks each day because your brain has only so much energy. As soon as you wake up, your brain begins to burn calories. When you make your first decision, you burn more calories and drain energy from your brain. Some studies indicate that by the time you get to the third task of the day, your brain is at 50 percent capacity.

Have you ever cruised through part of your day like a zombie and found it hard to concentrate? It's most likely because you've loaded yourself down with tasks that require too many decisions to the point you've drained your brain of so much energy that you're no longer effective.

Stop doing that.

It's important to think about your life holistically.

You try to break down your life according to career, family, friends, spiritual, and so on, but your mind doesn't work that way. What you experience at home you bring to work, and you take your stress from work back home.

Your life is one big, tangled mess of obstacles, challenges, and conflict. Your brain doesn't care if they're from work or home. It burns calories and energy to navigate those challenges.

You must protect it.

I first learned about the importance of priorities from Stephen Covey's book *The 7 Habits of Highly Effective People*, when his words challenged me to "put the first things first."

It's fine to have a list of tasks. What is not fine is to set yourself up for failure by trying to tackle a list that's way too daunting and then feeling guilty when you can't possibly complete it. Or worse, totally draining yourself by completing everything on your list at the cost of your mental, physical, and relational health.

I've tried many ways to focus and landed on paring down my task list to the three most important things I must complete each day.

Stephen Covey's wisdom taught me the importance of prioritizing, but Michael Hyatt and Daniel Harkavy's book *Living Forward* taught me the importance of life domains.

My big three couldn't be categorized to the three most important things at work, the three most important things at home, and so forth. They had to be the three most important things from all domains of life.

That paradigm shift was a game changer for me.

Before that moment, I'd carried around a task list for work, a separate list for my family, another list for myself, and so on. I stopped doing that and instead merged my list and focused on the most important items from a main list from then on, and it's made a world of difference.

One of my West Point professors once told me she went to bed every night by eight-thirty. That seemed lovely to me at the time, as a sleep-deprived cadet who never seemed to have enough time to fit everything into my schedule.

When I asked her how she fit it all in her day, she said, "I don't, and I don't worry about it. I can't possibly get it all done, and that's okay. My tasks will be waiting for me when I wake up the next day."

I yearned for that type of freedom, so I waited for a time in my life when I could do that as well.

It never came.

I had to be deliberate with my approach to my days, so I learned to take control of my life and build boundaries around my big three. I adapted to this mentality, and everything turned out fine. More than fine, in fact.

It's not easy. It will get messy as you make the transition to focusing on your big three, but don't fret because your life is messy anyway. You will settle, and things will get better.

So how do you get started with this mentality of focusing on your main things?

Embrace the Power of Next

There are many times that the whirlwind of life dominates your days. Life is one overwhelming experience to the next overwhelming experience. I had to embrace that I would never get time to settle; there was never a natural pause for rest.

The whirlwind of life can be relentless.

Beware of just working hard "for a season" because that season may never end. Your greatest tool to fight overwhelm is to use the power of next.

What's the very next thing you need to do that will move the needle in a meaningful way in your life? The next thing should be with one of your primary three tasks for the day.

Your boss or others may dictate your day. If you don't control your day, someone else will. It's critical to build boundaries with others. Do this by asking three clarifying questions when someone approaches you with a task:

- **How important is this?** This is a reasonable question to ask. Find out how important it is to the other person, and then assess where that fits within your priorities.

- **When do you need this?** Clarify the other person's expectation on when they need closure on the task.

- **What other important item would you prefer I take off my list to accommodate this new request?** This is a key question to ask when a supervisor or leader within your organization is asking you to complete a task. By doing this, you maintain control because you replace other tasks with this new, more important task so you can properly manage your day.

Embrace the Power of No

I look for common traits when studying successful people. Not only do successful people say no, but they say it a lot!

You simply cannot take on every task or accept every opportunity that comes your way. You need to get comfortable with declining many things in your life.

Life doesn't follow your rules. It doesn't abide by your timeline, and it doesn't care about your feelings. It just happens without your consent. The chaos of life is a variable you must contend with as you navigate the travails of daily living.

When dealt an unexpected blow, consider this methodology to deal with it:

- **Give yourself space to process it.** It's okay to pause and allow yourself time to get through the stunning effect of a turbulent event or circumstance.

- **Reevaluate your expectations.** Your plans going into a project didn't consider this unexpected issue. Do your expectations need to be adjusted?

- **Reevaluate your priorities.** Depending on the issue, you may need to adjust your priorities to account for it.

- **Adjust your mindset.** Evolve to accommodate the unexpected.

Everyone has a COVID-19 story.

As a public speaker who depends on live events where hundreds of people gather, I lost thousands of dollars in the first few weeks of the shutdown.

I had to evolve to survive.

I was forced to translate my message into a virtual environment, build a virtual studio, and learn how to connect with my audience in a virtual setting. It wasn't easy, and it drained me, but I figured it out and enjoyed a record-breaking year in revenue as a result.

Give yourself grace.

It's not easy to adjust. I had blowouts with my family while in lockdown. I was stressed. My family was stressed. Everyone was stressed. Conflict was inevitable. We had to forgive one another and figure it out, and we did.

Start building space in your life to account for the unexpected.

Many times, you won't complete your big three, and that's okay. Sometimes you just need to take a nap or binge watch a show. That's fine. Build space in your life for moments when you're not at your best.

Many times, you won't feel like you're winning at life, and all you can muster in the moment is to focus on what's next just to keep your head above water and not drown in a sea of chaos, and that's completely normal.

Just do the very next thing that makes sense to you, and the rest will take care of itself.

I challenge you to merge your task list into a main list. Review that list daily, and identify the three most important tasks you would like to complete each day. It doesn't always have to be three items; it can be one item for the day. Just no more than three.

Build the constraint of identifying your daily big three, and keep the Beast from overwhelming you with too many meaningless tasks that will do nothing but drain you and pull you from your path to significance.

Puzzle piece: For the next thirty days, identify your daily big three each day, and then do the next logical task on that list of three items.

Chapter 8

THE TRUTH ABOUT ENERGY

Perfect Day Element #2: Manage Your Energy

The energy of the mind is the essence of life.

—Aristotle

Disclaimer: I'm not a doctor, nor do I claim to be one. I'm going to share ideas to help with your energy. I recommend that you consult your doctor before you implement my advice. What I share in this chapter is what's working for me and may work for you, but it's not guaranteed.

"So how do you feel about twins?"

My jaw dropped, and my eyes widened to take in the sonogram picture that showed not one but two heads.

Alia and I were shocked but excited.

We'd always imagined our life with two boys in it. We even had names picked out: Ryan and Adrian. On the sonogram picture, our doctor gave them the names Baby A and Baby B. Even today, our daughter has those names loaded into her phone.

We made the decision that the first one born would be Ryan, and the second one would be Adrian. Funny how it works, as their names suit them well. Ryan, with his light hair and fair skin, looks Irish, and Adrian, with his dark, olive skin and jet-black hair, fits his name perfectly.

We were unprepared when we brought our firstborn, Ashley, home. That was nothing compared to how fundamentally unprepared we were when we brought our twin boys home. The first day we brought our boys home from the hospital, I picked my parents up from the Denver airport. When I arrived back home with them, I found Alia sitting on the floor with the boys. She was holding a bottle of formula in each of their mouths and had a look on her face that said, "What do I do now?"

That started a year of total and utter exhaustion that I had not experienced since my early days in the military. Life didn't slow down, and the boys' needs for constant care and attention were relentless.

One boy woke up in the middle of the night, and when we got that one down, the other woke up. The cycle continued all night. At first, we tried to tackle the overnight duties in shifts, like we did with Ashley, but that didn't work. We were both exhausted all the time.

We needed a new plan.

We decided to take weeklong shifts that required one parent to be exhausted for the week. One of us got up in the middle of the night to handle the kids while the other rested through the night. It was horrible for one of us during the week, but the other was able to rest and recover. It worked, and we got through it.

Once that first year settled down and the boys began to sleep through the night, Alia and I rediscovered a normal life where we both slept. After that first year, we came to the same conclusion.

We could face just about anything in life with a full night of sleep!

Several years ago, the popular battery brand Energizer had a famous commercial that demonstrated the power of its battery compared to the competition. To demonstrate this, Energizer launched a commercial campaign that showed its mascot, a toy bunny, with an exuberant amount of energy clamoring away compared to its competitors that couldn't last nearly as long because of an inferior battery life.

What the famous Energizer bunny commercials don't show you is that bunny doesn't last that long either because it's still powered by a battery that eventually runs out of juice.

Everything has a battery life, including you.

Before you can thrive in life, you must learn how to survive it.

Energy is a key component of survival. You must have energy to face the Beast and then to tame it. Your energy provides you with three fundamental, essential elements:

1. **Brain power.** This is your most important battery. Your brain needs an abundance of energy to perform.

2. **Physical power.** You need stores of energy to physically face the challenges of the day.

3. **Perspective power.** This is a key component to navigate life. To rise above your chaos, you need altitude, like an airplane rising above a storm cloud. Your altitude and how you view life rises and falls in direct proportion to how much energy you have at your disposal.

Do you struggle with energy?

Of course you do. We all do. It's not just about having energy. It's about storing as much energy as possible and then managing what you have in the most effective and productive way.

I've been told that I bring a high level of energy to life. I have six guidelines I follow to manage my energy.

Guideline #1: Get Sleep

This sounds simple enough, so why does our society struggle with it so much?

Studies recommend seven to eight hours of sleep each night for optimal performance. It's important for your physical, mental, and emotional health.

I once read that someone who hasn't slept for several days straight has the same negative cognitive effects as someone driving under the influence of alcohol.

Have you ever felt punch-drunk because you're so exhausted?

There can be a correlation between lack of sleep and weight management. Whenever I lack energy because of my sleep patterns, I search for quick and cheap sources of energy like candy, junk food, soda, or anything caffeinated. This usually provides a short-term boost, but I eventually crash.

It's hard to concentrate when your body and mind are exhausted.

I view life differently when I'm tired. I often become less positive and focus on the negative components of life. In those moments, I realize I just need some rest. I can worry about my challenges later. Often, a good night of sleep is all I need to gain a fresh and more positive perspective for my life.

So how do we achieve a healthy sleep habit that sets us up for success?

First, sleep requires commitment.

Our cultural norms revere highly successful and famous people who claim that part of their success is that they sleep less. That sounds good on the surface until you dig a little further into those people's lives and learn that they are mostly a mess. These people experience broken relationships and health issues. If you truly want to survive your life and ultimately thrive, then you must make sleep a priority.

The solution to improve sleep is to build a nightly routine.

Your body is wired to accept a routine. Like a machine, your body will learn a routine and adapt to it. Here are my thoughts on how to build sleep into your nightly routine:

Set a time for sleep. Pick a time that you plan to go to sleep, and build your routine with that bedtime in mind.

Stop snacking two hours before bed. Don't fuel your body right before bed so you're dealing with stomach issues or trying to rest when your body is actively processing food. I don't have scientific evidence around my two-hour rule, but it works for me. Discover what works for you.

Eliminate your news addiction. News is negative, and negativity leads to stress. When you're stressed, your body releases a hormone called cortisol that puts you in survival mode. That's not helpful when you're trying to calm down and prepare for rest. Let the news go. It will be waiting for you when you wake up the next morning. You need to protect your mind and spirit so you can rest.

No phone time one hour before bed. Your phone is a portal to wasted time. It gives you access to negative news, family problems, and friend issues through social media. For me, YouTube is a black hole into mindless time wasted watching irrelevant videos that steal precious time that could be used for sleeping.

Read or listen to a book. This activity brings your brain into a soft landing before bed. It can be challenging to turn off your brain, but reading relaxes. Listening to someone else's voice reading to you has the same effect.

Close out your mind from worry time. This is hard, but when those worrisome thoughts enter your mind, acknowledge them and replace them with something positive. This takes time to learn and develop. Don't get frustrated.

Guideline #2: Take Naps

When I lived in Europe, it was an eye-opener regarding how other cultures lived. Napping was one of those strange concepts for me. Many Europeans think Americans are silly with our work-all-day mantra.

Sleep isn't just for nighttime. Naps are also a key part of the day because they restore depleted energy and refresh the spirit. They're good for brain health and nourish a positive perspective.

In their book *Rest: Why You Get More Done When You Work Less*, Alex Sojung and Kim Pang cite several famous high achievers who utilized naps as an effective productivity tool. People like

Winston Churchill, Dwight D. Eisenhower, Douglas MacArthur, John F. Kennedy, Thomas Edison, and Frank Lloyd Wright were all consistent nappers.

I've learned that twenty to thirty minutes achieves the desired effect of replenishing the soul. If you want to nap, here are some things to think about as you install this into your daily routine:

Nap during low-energy moments of the day. Don't fight it. Embrace it!

Nap during similar times of the day. Your body will learn your rhythms and to crave your daily naps.

Eliminate interruptions. Turn off every digital device that could interrupt your rest.

Embrace breathing techniques. I've found that deep, slow, rhythmic breathing helps to calm my mind and spirit. It prepares my body for rest.

Check your worries at the door. Life's issues will be waiting for you when you're done. This can be difficult at first, but you'll learn to clear your mind and allow it to rest.

Don't worry if you don't fall asleep. The act of pausing and giving your body and soul a moment to reset is life giving. Your body will learn to sleep over time. Be patient.

Be consistent. Your body will learn to nap, and it will become an integral part of your day.

Start by taking a twenty-minute nap every day around the same time. Be creative and find places that allow you to rest. I took naps in my car in the parking lot at work. Sometimes I shut the door in my office, turned out the lights, and put my head down at my desk. Now that I work at home, I go to my bed and rest there.

Find your place, and give your body a chance to reset for twenty minutes each day.

Guideline #3: Work Within Your Natural Rhythms

Are you a morning, afternoon, or evening person?

Don't fight who you are. Instead, leverage your peak times by prioritizing your best work when you're at your best.

Start with your big three.

Focus on those most important items of the day during your peak energy moments. For me, my peak hours are between five o'clock in the morning and noon. I leverage my peak time to focus on thinking, planning, and creating new content.

I avoid meetings as much as possible during my peak time.

My low-energy time is between the hours of two and five in the afternoon. I try to take my naps during this time. I like to book meetings during this time because they don't require my best energy.

I also book my virtual speaking gigs during this low-energy time because whenever I engage my superpower, my body pulls from a special reserve of energy.

I'm useless after six. I schedule restful activities like being with my family, engaging in hobbies, or doing chores around the house.

What do you do if you're a night person and your work requires you to engage during the day?

I suggest a hybrid schedule.

This requires creativity and coordination with your supervisor and colleagues. Try experimenting with engaging in your work during the night hours once or twice a month. You may find that you're more productive and of more value to your work by engaging in this schedule.

Guideline #4: Exercise

Exercise affects energy management in a few ways:

- **Brain health.** Increasing blood flow increases oxygen, which is like food for your brain. Why wouldn't you do something that would help you with your single greatest asset—your brain?

- **Peak performance**. Exercise trains your body for stamina, which prepares you for the stresses of life. Your body will pull from that training during a long project or anything in life that requires stamina to succeed.

- **Mood booster.** Exercise boosts your mood. How do you feel after you exercise? If you're like me, you feel fantastic, like you've done something good, which in turn makes you feel good.

I define exercise as anything that requires you to move your body. Walking, running, swimming, riding, standing up for longer periods of time—it doesn't matter.

Get your body out of the sitting position and engage in life.

Try some form of exercise for thirty minutes every day for a month and see how you feel.

Guideline #5: Drink Water

I've read that most Americans are dehydrated.

In fact, it may be as high as 75 percent of adult Americans are dehydrated at some point in the day.

The chances are, you're dehydrated right now. Does your mouth feel a little dry at this moment?

Stop right now. Pour yourself a tall glass of refreshing water, and take a long drink. Doesn't that feel nice?

There are some studies that suggest dehydration may be the primary culprit for midday fatigue. Feeling a little tired? Could it be because your body lacks the fluids it needs to be at peak performance?

Dehydration may cause foggy memory and lack of concentration. It can also affect your mood.

The solution is quite simple: drink more water. I adopted the guideline of drinking half my body weight in ounces of water. If you weigh 170 pounds, then that would require eighty-five ounces of water. You would drink around eleven cups each day, assuming the average cup is eight ounces.

Start each day by drinking a glass of water, and then commit to drinking half your body weight in ounces of water every day.

Guideline #6: Work Within Your Strengths

This might seem obvious, but simply working within your superpower gives you energy.

When you work within your natural talents, your body, mind, and soul become aligned because you're doing what you were meant to do.

Working where you're strong is fun. It's exciting to conquer tasks so easily.

It's easy to find energy reserves for things that excite you, and what's more exciting than doing what you love the most?

I call this my happy place.

Find your happy place, and live there as much as possible throughout your day.

Let's discuss your reality. Maybe your current reality or season of life is challenging right now. I get that. For instance, I'm able to do more things now because I have more freedom than I did when my kids were toddlers.

Acknowledge your current reality and embrace it. Then take the next logical step toward a more energized life.

You don't have to do everything I recommend at once. Pick one thing and focus on that until you master it. Then pick another and so on. Before you know it, you'll be full of energy and ready to take on the Beast. It won't stand a chance.

Now it's time to graduate from survival mode and into the world of success. There's plenty of room here. Come and join me.

Puzzle piece: Focus on your energy by choosing one of the six guidelines of managing your energy and spend time mastering it. Once you do that, pick another of the guidelines. Continue this pattern until you've mastered all six guidelines of managing your energy.

Chapter 9

WHY ONLY THE STRONG CAN THRIVE

Perfect Day Element #3: Work Within Your Strengths

Don't confuse activity with achievement.

—John Wooden

I WAS THRILLED TO MOVE INTO OUR NEW HOME IN BLOOMINGTON, Indiana, in 2010. It was the start of a new phase of life. The first few times I pulled into our driveway, I noticed a beautiful rosebush planted at the base of the mailbox.

The rosebush was in full bloom with its beautiful pink flowers. It was the first visual I saw when I entered the neighborhood and pulled into the driveway. I enjoyed seeing that bush, and I decided to maintain it so it would thrive the next year. Eventually, the petals fell, and the bush withered as it capitulated to the winter season.

I don't claim to have a green thumb. I only spend time in my yard handling basic upkeep on the bushes and other landscaping so that my home is presentable to the public. I wasn't sure what to do with that bush and thought maybe it had just died and that was it.

One afternoon, during a visit with my parents, my mom mentioned the bush.

"When do you plan to prune that rosebush for the season?" she asked.

"What do you mean?" I inquired.

"Well, you need to cut away those dead stems to make way for the new ones in the spring."

I had no idea I was supposed to do that. So that day, I went out to prune the rosebush, and when the spring came later that year, the bush thrived and out came those beautiful pink roses later in the summer.

I was ecstatic.

I've taken care of that little bush for the past decade, and I revel in its beauty every year.

Your life is like that rosebush. Your daily routine must be pruned so that you may continue to survive and thrive during your "winter" season.

What must you prune?

Your weaknesses.

Consider eliminating the things that fill your days and pull you away from a life of significance. To achieve success, you must create margin in your life and space in your soul that allows your superpower to thrive and bloom, just like my little rosebush.

You create that space by shedding the things that are unnecessary in your life: things that drain you or things that others can do just as well as you, if not better than you, and things that distract you.

The Beast uses these meaningless tasks to give you the illusion that you're achieving something, but you're really busy doing nothing. Stop spinning your wheels with unnecessary tasks. It's time to get back on track.

Before we discuss shedding your weaknesses any further, I want to address the difference between a moral weakness and a skill-set weakness.

It's not okay to neglect a moral issue. For instance, I used to struggle with my temper. It was a weakness that I could not ignore because it affected my family. I had to overcome it. You must do the same if you struggle with a moral weakness.

When it comes to skillsets, make a list of the daily activities you pursue, and label each task with the following properties:

- **Superpower.** You are uniquely qualified to do this task. It's a natural talent. For me, it's any task related to being a father, husband, or son. It's also related to anything to do with creating new content and delivering it on various platforms.

- **Draining.** Things that you despise and that sap your energy. This is paperwork, project management, administrative, and logistical work for me.

- **Others.** Things that others can do just as well as you, if not better. This involves any type of handiwork for me. It's also video editing, website development, and social media.

- **Distraction.** Things that you enjoy doing but others can do just as well, or things that are meaningless but you do to fill time in your day anyway. For me, it's business finances, email processing, and meeting coordination. It's also things like organizing my office or sorting through mail.

Next, scan your list and decide how you plan to shed some of those weak areas that are stunting your growth toward significance. Identify a potential action to take with each task that's not designated as a superpower.

Here are the possible action items:

- **Eliminate.** Is the task even necessary? Maybe there was a season for this task, but it's no longer viable, and it's just taking up mental space. Get rid of it.

- **Delegate.** Can you delegate this task to someone else? It may be a weakness for you but a strength for someone else. For instance, I hired a virtual assistant to handle all my travel. She books all my flights, hotels, and rental cars. She used to be an event planner, so she enjoys the work.

- **Trade.** Sometimes trading a task is your best option. You unload a weak task and in turn take on another task that lies within your strength. For instance, I had a colleague, Bill, who was exceptionally good with Microsoft Excel spreadsheets. Whenever I needed support on a spreadsheet, I called Bill, and he built it for me. In turn, Bill needed help with his budget approval process. I was good at developing proposals for budget line items, so I helped Bill build his proposals.

Once you begin to shed your weaknesses, you free up space to focus on activities within your passions and superpowers so you work within your power zone more often and get back on track toward significance.

Puzzle piece: Review your list of tasks and shed as many as you can. Shed the tasks that are draining, tasks that are distractions, and tasks others can do better.

Chapter 10

CLARITY IS EVERYTHING

Perfect Day Element #4: Live with Clarity

We can easily forgive a child who is afraid of the dark; the real tragedy of life is when men are afraid of the light.

—PLATO

SWEAT FLOODED MY VISION, AND I STRUGGLED TO CATCH MY breath.

"We're pinned down!" I heard my second squad leader yell from an abandoned building across the street.

"Enemy, eleven o'clock, fifty meters!" my driver yelled in my ear as we took cover on the first floor of a two-story building.

My head spun and my thoughts clouded as I attempted to calm my mind and contemplate our next move.

"What are you doing, Lieutenant?" Captain Bagget yelled.

This was our first training exercise after returning from Bosnia, a military operation in urban terrain (MOUT) exercise. The opposing force had stolen our anti-tank guided missile (AT4) system from our unit, and it was our mission to retrieve it. I carefully created a plan for my platoon to complete this mission, but our progress was slowed by enemy fire and obstacles set by the opposing force in the mock town. I became confused.

"Lieutenant, what's your mission?" Captain Bagget screamed above the chaos.

I took a deep breath and considered my primary objective. "To retrieve the stolen AT4!" I yelled back.

"Right. So what the hell are you doing?" Captain Bagget responded.

I paused and thought for a moment. Then I looked toward the ceiling and spotted the stolen AT4.

I recovered the AT4 and coordinated a hasty exit from the town, leaving the enemy behind. During the after-action review with Captain Bagget and my squad leaders, we discussed what had pulled us away from our mission and what we could do better next time.

The primary lesson we learned from that exercise was to maintain clarity of the mission and not to let the fog of battle pull us away from that mission. When my unit took on enemy fire, I was distracted from my mission, and I focused too much on the enemy.

I lost clarity.

An effective tactic the Beast will use against you is the "fog of war." Life can often seem like a battle of obstacles, problems, conflict, and pain all meant to do one thing: steal your clarity.

It's easy to get busy, fill your life with activity, and become distracted from your true path.

I was afraid to face my true path. I chose a path of fruitless activity, where I was busy doing nothing and getting nowhere, because I lacked a vision for my life.

I lacked clarity.

Once I opened my eyes, I found my path. I thought I needed all the answers, when in fact I needed clarity on only certain key areas to start moving in the right direction.

The same is true for you.

A critical year for me was 2000. I spent a lot of time with my mentor, Howie. I absorbed so much from him, and his wisdom planted seeds in my heart that became profoundly useful a few years later.

One evening, Howie asked a group of us, "What's your favorite day of the week?"

I thought about it, and Saturday came to mind.

He pulled a marble from his pocket and presented it to the group. "Let's pretend this marble represents your favorite day."

I stared at the marble and listened intently.

"Now let's pretend we know that each of you will pass away on your eightieth birthday. If this marble represents your favorite day, how many days do you have left?"

I quickly did the math. If I passed away at the age of eighty, I would have 2,340 Saturdays left.

"Now, Saturday is my favorite day. Why do we buy into the fact that we must live a life where there's a Monday, a Tuesday, a Wednesday, a Thursday, a Friday, a Saturday, and a Sunday?" Howie asked the group.

"What if you changed your entire paradigm, the way you approached your days, such that you lived a life that today was a Saturday, tomorrow was a Saturday, and the day after that was a Saturday? What if you lived a life where you had six Saturdays and a Sunday?"

Howie held up the marble for effect.

"If you changed your perspective and began to live your life differently so you lived a life of six Saturdays and a Sunday, how many Saturdays would you have left?" Howie asked the group.

I did the math. If I did what Howie suggested, I would have 14,040 Saturdays left!

"How fired up would you be about your life if you lived like that?" he inquired.

Howie scanned the room at the young people listening to him. He made eye contact with each of us.

"What is it about your favorite day that makes it so special to you? What is it about that day that you love so much?" he asked.

For me, Saturday represented freedom.

It was the one day of the week that allowed me to pursue everything I desired. I was able to go on long runs deep in the woods. I enjoyed satisfying breakfasts at the local breakfast joint. I took long naps in the afternoon and pursued hobbies I enjoyed. I explored unknown places, like small towns hosting unique festivals.

Most of all, I created new content.

I penned stories. I liked to write and to get things out of my head and onto paper. I loved being creative, and I tapped into that passion only on my weekends.

Howie broke the long silence and interrupted my thoughts. "I challenge you to change your paradigm and create a life that allows you to pursue the things you love, the things that are meaningful to you. Stop living a life where you put the most important things into a little box that's opened and enjoyed only one day a week."

That wisdom started me down a path of discovering a way of life that allowed me to live my six Saturdays and a Sunday.

That day, Howie gave me the gift of perspective.

Are you living your life with clarity?

It's not about the time you have. It's more about what you do with the time you're given with clarity and a healthy perspective. If you desire to live your life where you focus on the main thing every day, not just once a week, then you must clarify your personal vision.

A Personal Vision

Everyone should have a personal vision for their life. There are two levels of vision: short term (three to five years) and long term (five to ten years).

A clear vision informs your decisions. It's easier to make decisions when you know where you want to go with your life. Don't worry if you're not clear on where you want to be five years from now. How about this time next year?

Your vision will evolve and grow as you do. Write it in pencil and be willing to edit it along the way. The main thing is to get it on paper. If you're not sure how to do this, start by writing a letter to yourself and date it one year from today. Write the letter in present tense and be specific.

What do you want life to look like one year from today?

Don't overthink this exercise, and don't worry about how you plan to accomplish your vision. That comes later. For now, get clear on where you want to go with your life. The first step to rise above chaos is to gain clarity on your destination.

Eventually, you will graduate to crafting a five-year and ten-year vision. Here's my vision for my life:

> I'm a highly sought-after professional speaker. I'm touring the country speaking and teaching from my bestselling books *Rise above Chaos* and *The 21st Mile*.
>
> Ashley has her associate's degree and is starting her career in event planning. Ryan is going into his second year in college running varsity cross-country and track. Adrian is heading into his second year at West Point.
>
> Alia and I moved into our waterfront home in a small, coastal town in South Carolina, and we're enjoying life with our two Dobermans, Oynx and Roman.

A Personal Mission

A well-crafted mission is the vehicle that gets you where you want to go and helps you realize your vision for your life. A mission is an overarching central activity you pursue to achieve your vision.

Your mission will provide you with the gift of focus. Here's an example of my personal mission:

> In the next five years, I will help 10,000 busy professional men and women rediscover their passion so that they can redefine their purpose and gain the courage to act. By doing this, they will live in peace knowing they are leading a life of significance.

A Purpose

Your purpose fuels your journey and gives you the strength and courage to live out your mission. You find your purpose when you align your passion with your superpower and daily activities. It's hard to stop a person living a life on purpose, even for the Beast. Remember:

(PASSION+SUPERPOWER)*ACTION = PURPOSE

Here's my purpose statement:

> I'm a professional speaker, and my purpose is to communicate hope and assist my audience in finding a path to pursue their own version of significance. The action I take to ensure I live

out my purpose is to consistently reach out to event planners who may consider hiring me to speak at their events.

Personal Value

To live out a life on purpose, you must clarify your value to the world.

First, consider what others perceive as your value. I'm not advocating for allowing the world to determine your value. I'm advocating for you to gain awareness about how others perceive your value. This helps you identify any gaps you must fill with your purposeful activities.

For instance, just because I decided to become a professional speaker didn't mean people were lining up to hire me. I had to earn the right to speak on stage. I took deliberate steps to become a paid speaker. I invested countless hours learning the art of professional speaking, traveled thousands of miles to conferences across the country, and spoke for free many times before I found the first organization willing to pay me.

Everyone goes through an amateur phase on their way to living out their true value. Your true value equals your superpower.

Here's where I landed on my superpower:

> My superpower is that I can simplify a topic, develop content on that topic, and deliver the content to an audience in a way that's fun, engaging, and easy to consume.

Your Reality

No one escapes this. We all have a reality that we must embrace. It could be health, financial, family, community, or a combination of several things. The first step on this journey is to acknowledge your reality. By doing this, you take power away from the Beast.

The good news is that once you acknowledge your reality, you can take steps to manipulate it so that it elevates you instead of holding you back from significance.

How do you do it?

Let go of your own issues and focus on others.

Something magical happens when you take your eyes off yourself and serve others. You gain perspective on life and your own problems as you begin to help others solve their problems. You begin to look at your own challenges in a different way and find creative ways to live out your life.

Here's the best way to serve others:

- **Identify obstacles and problems.** What are others suffering from, or what are their pain points?

- **Bring solutions by leveraging your superpower.** Don't try to solve problems unless they allow you to leverage your strengths.

- **Ease the burden of others.** Life is hard. Look for ways to ease someone else's pain.

Be patient in your relationships with others. John Maxwell, in his book *Winning with People*, introduces his idea known as the boomerang principle, which states, "When we help others, we help ourselves."

Don't be entitled. The world owes you nothing. Help others, not because of what they can do for you in return but because you genuinely want to help them succeed.

Everything else will work out on its own.

Puzzle piece: Clarify your vision for your life by writing a letter to yourself and dating it one year from today. Write it in present tense and capture what you want your life to look like in a year. Once you're finished with the letter, put it in a sealed envelope and mark on your calendar to read that letter back to yourself in one year.

Chapter 11

THE TRUTH ABOUT CONFLICT

Perfect Day Element #5: Manage Expectations

Through many dangers, toils, and snares, I have already come; 'Tis grace has brought me safe thus far and grace will lead me home.

—JOHN NEWTON

I DON'T BELIEVE IN THE HONEYMOON STAGE IN A MARRIAGE. I think it's a lie. Alia and I didn't experience a honeymoon stage. In fact, the hardest part of our two-decade marriage, thus far, was those first few years.

We argued about everything as we struggled to settle into our roles and figure each other out. We even argued over something as simple as riding bikes!

One afternoon, I approached my friend and mentor, Jeff, about my plight.

"Dude, what's wrong with my marriage? We can't even go on a bike ride without it turning into an all-out brawl by the end of it," I explained over lunch.

Jeff smiled and listened intently as I pored over everything that was wrong with my relationship with Alia at the time.

"Let's go back to your bike ride for a moment," Jeff said, stopping my rant. "Have you ever asked Alia what she wants to get out of the ride with you?"

"Um, no. Isn't it obvious?" I shrugged my shoulders.

Jeff laughed. "Do yourself a favor. Before your next ride, ask your wife what her expectations are for the ride. You might be surprised by what she says."

The next week, Alia and I pulled out our bikes for a Saturday afternoon ride. I took Jeff's advice and asked, "Hey, can I ask you something?"

Alia nodded without making eye contact as she adjusted her biking helmet.

"What's your goal for this ride today?"

"That's the problem," she quipped.

"What's the problem?" I snapped back at her.

"I don't want there to be a goal. I just want to ride and enjoy it."
She held up her arms in protest.

"You're not enjoying our rides?" I asked defensively.

"No, I'm not." Alia frowned at me and pointed at my watch on my
wrist. "For starters, leave that stupid watch at home. Who cares
how long it takes to complete our ride? Everything doesn't have
to be a competition, you know."

"Okay, I get it. No watch. Anything else?" I softened my tone.

"Let's just ride to be riding. It doesn't have to be a workout. Who
cares if we sweat? Can't we just ride for fun?" she responded,
raising the tone of her voice.

"I'm sorry. I didn't know it was an issue," I stated.

"Really? How could you not know it was an issue?" she protested.

"Okay, okay, I get it. No watch, no competition, no sweat. Like,
truly, it's no sweat!" I smiled.

It was a pleasant ride that day and has turned into one of our
favorite activities to do as a couple, all because I had the courage
to ask her expectations for the ride.

The first step toward connecting with others is managing expectations. You spend the bulk of your life working with others in

your chosen profession. Studies show that work will be a source of stress for you mainly because of your coworkers.

- Up to 80 percent of work difficulties are a result of strained relationships.

- Up to 40 percent of a manager's time is spent with conflict management.

- Around 25 percent of workers call in sick to avoid conflict at work.

Expectations are the primary source of most conflict.

When you fail to properly manage your own expectations and the expectations of others, you can expect conflict. It can be as simple as going on a bike ride with your spouse or as complex as solving a major community problem with civic leaders.

In the end, success with others always comes down to expectations.

I've discovered four guidelines of expectation management.

Guideline #1: Be Proactive

Meeting others' expectations starts with you.

How's your stress level? Your stress level influences how you see the world, which dictates whom you attract.

Do you like whom you've surrounded yourself with lately?
If not, could it be you're attracting exactly who you are?

Self-awareness is a critical first step in human dynamics. It starts with acknowledging your level of stress and making the necessary adjustments to mitigate stress so it doesn't impact your relationships.

What do you seek?

Whatever you seek, you can find. I can visit your community and find despair, abuse, corruption, racism, or almost any evil thing I desire to find. I can also find hope, love, strong community, charity, healthy families, and servanthood.

You find what you're looking for, so what are you looking for today?

John Eldridge introduced me to Dunbar's number in his book *Getting Your Life Back*. Dunbar's number is based on a study done in the 1990s by anthropologist Robin Dunbar who suggests a person has the capacity to maintain 150 stable relationships.

You're limited in your capacity to empathize with others.

Connecting with others is the key to significance, but it's also draining and overwhelming. Being aware of your capacity to connect with others and being willing to pause and step away from humanity to replenish your relationship tank is important to your well-being.

I pause every morning by reading and writing for at least an hour. Every Sunday morning, I spend thirty minutes reflecting on and journaling about the previous week. This strategic pause helps me to regain perspective and reset my expectations of myself and others.

Learn to pause and step away from the world. More importantly, step away from all the relationships you're trying to manage so that you can refresh your spirit and maintain a healthy perspective.

Guideline #2: Be Clear with Your Expectations

Most relationships struggle because of fuzzy or implied expectations. Stop assuming people know what you want from them. Gain the courage to have conversations with key stakeholders in your life to identify gaps in expectations.

Ask these clarifying questions when connecting with others:

- **What are your expectations of that person?**

- **What are their expectations of you?**

- **Where are the gaps in expectations?**

Once you identify a gap in expectations, it's your responsibility to close it so you can have a healthy and meaningful experience with that person.

Michael Hyatt taught me how to mitigate conflict caused by a gap in expectations by asking a powerful question:

What must be true?

It's a beautiful question because it allows the other person the freedom to express what conditions must be in place to meet their expectations.

In the case of my bike-riding summit with my wife, her answer to that question was that the ride needed to be about the experience and less about a workout. Just being together and enjoying each other's company was the goal.

I needed a workout to challenge my cardiovascular system. The solution was for me to go on a solo ride before Alia and I rode together. I could get in my workout, and by the time it was over, I was ready to ride with Alia for fun.

We both won in this scenario because we were able to answer the question, "What must be true?"

Guideline #3: Be Predictable with Your Emotions

Do you have a person in your life who is unpredictable emotionally? How do you feel about that relationship? Do you enjoy walking on eggshells when you're with that person? Of course you don't enjoy that relationship. No one enjoys an emotionally unstable relationship.

Can others count on you to be predictable?

Relationships are built on a foundation of trust, and predictability breeds trust. People need to know what they will get out of you emotionally. I'm not talking about being fake with people because I want you to be authentic. Just be consistent with your behavior.

I have several close friends who are naturally grumpy, and I cherish them. They're good people, and I can count on them for support and guidance. I don't need them to be happy and cheery; I need them to be real. I cherish them not because they're constantly peppy but because they add value to me, and I add value to them. We have a mutually beneficial relationship that's built on trust because we can count on each other to be predictable.

Be authentic and pick an emotional lane so you attract the right group of people who value you as a person and what you bring to the world. You must commit to your relationships and know it takes time.

Embrace the fact that you may add more value to others than you will receive in return. The key is to add value within your superpower. When you do that, you won't resent it because it's fun to work within your strengths.

Guideline #4: Start with the Most Respected Person

Time is at a premium, and you don't have the luxury to manage expectations with everyone in your life, so start with the most respected person within your network. Narrow your focus to your top five most important people.

When you interact with your five most important people, be curious with them. Ask good questions, and find out what they desire and what's important to them. Then add value to them by leveraging your strengths. By doing this, you will form strong connections that will lead to long-lasting relationships.

In the fall of 2000, I went to my first Customer Connections Conference, an event hosted by the American Public Power Association (APPA). It started an eighteen-year journey that finally landed me as the closing keynote speaker at that very same conference in 2019.

I tried to be their keynote speaker for several years. I served the event planners by helping them find speakers for their agenda. I served on committees to decide on the agenda. I served as a breakout session speaker and preconference workshop presenter. I did this all for free until finally they decided to hire me as their closing speaker.

I remember the feeling of stepping out on the stage at the hotel in downtown New Orleans to close out the conference. I looked out into the crowd and saw many friendly faces of people I served and supported for several years. I also remember the standing ovation I received from those very same people. It felt extremely satisfying because I knew it was in recognition of eighteen years of relationship building.

I would do it all over again because I gained many friendships and valuable experiences while serving others on my way to that stage. It was a lesson in how community works. A community is not meant to serve an individual but to add value to the whole. I played my role with discipline and humility, and the community rewarded me for it.

Your community will reward you, too. You must be willing to invest in it.

Conflict is inevitable, so expect it. The cure for conflict is the proper management of expectations. Once you get comfortable managing expectations, it's time to be intentional with assembling your team.

This is when your journey to significance gets exciting!

Puzzle piece: Identify your five most important relationships. Clarify the expectations of those key relationships by answering the three expectation questions listed under Guideline #2 in this chapter.

Chapter 12

THE IMPORTANCE OF A TEAM

Perfect Day Element #6: Assemble a Team

Alone we can do so little; together we can do so much.

—HELEN KELLER

DARYL, MY FUTURE BROTHER-IN-LAW AND FIRSTIE (SENIOR) AT the United States Military Academy, sat with me in my living room. It was early summer 1991, and I was days away from heading off to West Point to start a new adventure.

"The next few months will be hard for you. You'll get through it, but not by doing it alone. You're going to need your classmates to survive, so embrace them and serve them, and they will serve you. Together with your classmates, you'll make it on the other side," said Daryl.

He was right.

To say I struggled in those first few weeks at the academy is an understatement. Each day was worse than the previous one, and I was on a fast track to failure.

That's when I met Jack.

Jack was a recruited runner from Georgia. He was my classmate and teammate. We were both a few days removed from freshly shaved heads and both reeling from our first moments at West Point.

We were in shock.

Our only respite was a few hours of "mass athletics." This was when we were allowed to spend time with our teammates and coaches down at the indoor track and field. Our coaches allowed us that time to relax and escape from the stress of being a new cadet.

Jack approached me at the very first session. His eyes revealed his stress. His face was tense, and his lips quivered. "Hey, man. We've got to stick together, or we're not going to make it."

It was a simple statement of despair from a young man I'd just met, but I agreed. We connected in that moment because we knew we needed the support of each other to make it. Jack was the first of several new cadets I connected with to survive that summer.

West Point sets cadets up for failure.

The system overloads each new cadet with so many duties and tasks that it's truly impossible to succeed without teamwork. The academy instills the need for a team from day one and hammers that point throughout the cadet experience.

Luckily, I connected with my teammates for survival, and over time those relationships strengthened, and I cherished them.

Jack became more than my classmate and teammate; he became my brother. We supported each other throughout our time at West Pont and beyond. He stood next to me at my wedding. He sat and cried with me when my sister passed away, and he is one of the first people I call when I need advice.

Jack is one of several key team members who support me on my path to significance.

Living a life of significance is impossible without the help of others. To achieve significance, you must be selective and intentional with whom you surround yourself for support. If you desire to win at life, then you must first win with people because your relationships are the foundation of your success.

Our society celebrates loners.

Movies and entertainment romanticize heroes who "go it alone." Rambo fights his foes by himself in the cover of darkness. Pick any old western with Clint Eastwood or John Wayne as its main character, and he's almost always fighting his battles alone.

But the term "lone wolf" is a fallacy.

Wolves don't navigate the wild alone. They survive because they hunt in packs. Their primal instincts demand that they roam together because there's strength and safety in numbers.

Life is too hard and exhausting to face alone. You need edifying and supporting relationships to face the Beast.

Whom are you doing life with?

I recommend you assemble a team or a group of individuals who support a common vision and leverage one another's strengths. A healthy team has the best interests of each member in mind.

A team can be made up of informal and formal relationships, and it's relevant to your phase of life. You don't have to have a formal title or a promotion to assemble a team. You only need the desire and wisdom to do so.

A team leverages each team member's resources and strengths to maximize the team's output. Your team members provide you with perspective because they ease the burdens of your daily life, which gives you space and the freedom to focus on the main things.

Your team also holds you accountable to a higher standard that forces you to level up your life. Your team covers your weaknesses so that you may focus on your strengths. Your teammates pick you up when you're down and provide support and love when you stumble in your journey.

Be the kind of person who attracts the right people. Would you want to be on your team? Are you aware of your flaws? Do you need to clean up some things in your life so that you can attract and maintain strong, healthy relationships?

This was a big one for me.

When I evaluated my life when I hit my rock bottom in 2005, I realized I didn't really like myself or what I had become. I wouldn't have wanted to interact with me. I needed to change.

Most likely, you won't require big, sweeping changes to how you approach life—just a few tweaks. For instance, I needed to learn to listen more. I needed to value others' opinions and consider their perspectives. It was hard at first, but I developed better listening skills. I realized that just because I have an opinion doesn't mean I have to express it all the time. I began to filter my words and became more measured in my responses to others.

Evaluate your approach and interaction with others, and look for some tweaks you can make that will make you easier to connect with in the future.

When assembling a team, there are four types of team members you will engage with as you pursue significance:

1. **Opinion leaders** are people who have the ability to influence others' thoughts and opinions. When they opine on a particular topic, people listen. They protect you, counsel you, and open doors for you.

2. **Champions** are your cheerleaders. They build you up and cheer you on when you need them the most. Their support for you is unconditional.

3. **Difference makers** have specific skillsets that you need because you lack them but need them to succeed. They're strong where you are weak.

4. **Decision makers** have the power to make decisions and the financial resources to back them up. They have budget authority and can provide valuable resources to your projects.

There's no magic mix of these team members other than you need at least one opinion leader and one decision maker on your team. You can have as many difference makers and champions as you'd like.

When assembling a team, there are three primary guidelines to follow.

Guideline #1: Awareness

What phase of life are you in now?

Each phase has a different set of challenges that require specific team members to help you get through it. For example, early in our marriage, Alia and I needed a strong group of caregivers to help us raise our young children.

Embrace your strengths and move away from your weaknesses. Assemble a team that allows you to focus on your strengths 80 percent of the time. This doesn't happen overnight. It takes time to cover your weaknesses, so be patient.

Guideline #2: Attract the Right Team Members

My mentor, Howie, once told me, "I know your future based on the books you read and the people you hang out with."

Howie encouraged me to fill my mind with positive information. He gave me a goal to read for fifteen minutes every day. This allowed me to grow intellectually and expand my paradigm that attracted others to me.

Listen to podcasts or books while exercising or traveling. Seek out powerful training events to learn from others and network with good people. You will find potential team members at these events.

The reason these growth-minded activities are important is that as you read and grow, you'll begin to clarify your thinking, and your path to significance will begin to form in front of you. This will formulate your vision for the future.

The more you grow, the greater the clarity you gain from that growth. Quality people and high achievers are attracted to people with clarity and vision. If you want to surround yourself with rock stars, gain clarity in your life. This starts with feeding your mind with positive information every day.

Identify what you need in terms of human connection and potential team support in these primary areas in your life:

- Spiritual

- Marriage

- Wealth

- Health

- Work

- Hobbies

Some of those areas may require more attention than others, and the attention required in a particular area may change as you grow in your life. The key is to be aware of which area requires support and assemble teammates to help you in that area. For instance, wealth is a big deal to me in this phase of my life. I've created a strong cash flow in my speaking business, so I've surrounded myself with people who understand finances and wealth-building so they can counsel me on what to do to ensure I build for the future.

Guideline #3: Prune Your Relationships

I once had a mentor tell me you become the average of your five closest friends. So if that's true, who are your five closest friends?

The people you spend the most time with are the ones who influence your paradigm.

I struggled with this for a few years while supporting my daughter's softball activities. I began to spend more time with coaches and parents associated with the sport.

These were not my people, but I spent many hours with them over long weekends during the summers. I found myself agitated and more negative by the end of the season. My daughter began to experience a similar situation with some of the players. This continued for a few years until finally, my daughter and I agreed it was time to move on from the sport and separate ourselves from that environment.

It wasn't all the parents, players, and coaches associated with softball who were causing us issues, but it was enough that it influenced our attitudes and behavior, and we decided it was time to make a change.

There was a sense of profound relief once we let go of those relationships and decided to move on from them.

If you don't like the world you perceive, could it be the result of the people you've allowed into your life?

What do they mean to you? What kind of message are you projecting based on the friends you keep? How do you feel about your friendships?

If your friends influence your paradigm and your paradigm attracts others, who are you attracting?

It's important to be intentional with whom you attract to your inner circle. When you lean into this concept, I recommend you follow this methodology:

Evaluate your friendships. This can be a difficult exercise because you have history and emotional connections with those you've spent your life with.

But not all friendships are equipped to last a lifetime.

Perhaps you've held on to some relationships for too long. Those relationships were meaningful for a season, but has that season passed? Is it time to move on from some of your relationships?

Identify influencers. These relationships are the cornerstones of your significance path because these folks influence you and those around you. They're game changers and highly successful. When you develop a relationship with an influencer, cherish it. Nurture these relationships because they are the most valuable assets you have.

Add value to the right people. The world is filled with others who are on journeys and need support. Add value to the people with whom you wish to build relationships by leveraging your superpower to help them. For example, if you're good with numbers, support a colleague who needs help evaluating a complicated spreadsheet.

You also add value with the sacrifice of your time. Time is your most precious asset. When you give your time to another, you edify that person and strengthen the relationship. Invest time in people who matter to you.

Enjoy the value of reciprocity. Healthy relationships are symbiotic. They work because each party receives value from the connection. When you support someone, they are inspired to do the same for you.

Cardinal Rules for Healthy Relationships

Once you attract the right people to your team, you must continually maintain and grow those relationships. I follow these three rules:

Rule #1: Be curious.

Ask good questions and maintain a desire to learn about others' needs, wants, and desires:

- What gets them excited?

- What do they value?

- What are their passions?

The more you learn about your teammates, the easier it becomes to support them because you understand their journey.

Rule #2: Be relational.

It's important that you maintain a relational spirit with your team. Don't get caught up in being transactional with them. This means don't just take from them to support only your goals. Be willing to pause and step away from the grind to nurture the relationships. Once a quarter, I take account of my most important relationships and ask myself, "What were my last three interactions with this person?" If they're all transactional, then I know I have work to do.

Rule #3: Be organized.

Respect people's time. Being organized is important when it comes to asking people for their time. Here's what I focus on when it comes to being organized with my team:

- **Show up on time and leave early.** My mother, a highly successful entrepreneur and master relationship builder, once told me, "If you leave before they're ready for you to leave, then they'll always want you back." There's wisdom in this statement. Never overstay your welcome. If you promised a thirty-minute phone call, don't drag it on for forty-five minutes.

- **Be clear and concise.** People are busy. Most folks don't have the time or energy to deal with fuzzy, messy, or implied communication. Many folks don't have the patience for long, drawn-out correspondence. Get to the point, especially with influencers.

- **Follow up.** If you commit to something, do it. If you identify something that requires follow-up, do it. Don't leave things undone, unfulfilled, or open-ended. Seek closure in all things when relating with your team.

- **Communicate.** Relationships don't fail because of overcommunication. They fail because of the wrong communication. Be clear and concise in your communication, and communicate often with those within your team. I engage in regular check-ins with key relationships. They're not long and drawn-out interactions, but they are powerful and very necessary.

Questions for a Healthy Team

Once you've assembled your team and fallen into a nice rhythm to maintain your relationships, how do you manage the team as a whole?

Here are the questions I ask to help me keep my team intact:

- **Are the right people in the right spots?** You can recruit the right people, but it won't matter unless those people are set up to leverage their strengths to support your vision.

- **Do they want to be on your team?** If not, then you must get this person off your team. This can be frustrating because they might be a perfect fit on your team, but for whatever reason, they're not interested. Move on from this person.

- **Are they qualified to do what you're asking them to do?** If not, then you need to fill this gap with mentorship, more training, or tools. Do whatever is necessary to get them qualified.

Getting Others to Join You

Just because you've identified folks you want to do life with doesn't mean they will join you on the journey. They may need some convincing first. Here's the best approach:

- **Clarify the problem.** Explain what problem you're trying to solve. For me, it's helping others find their path to significance. Everyone on my team has a role in that mission.

- **Present your solution.** Clearly communicate how you plan to solve that problem. Everyone on my team knows the various ways I help others find their significance. This very book you're reading is an excellent example. I needed plenty of help from my team to develop and launch this book so you could have the chance to read it.

- **State the desired outcome.** Show your team what will happen because of the solution. What's the promise of transformation? People are inspired by transformation.

- **Demonstrate why you are the right person.** Just because you clearly define the problem, solution, and transformation doesn't mean your team believes you're the right person to lead the effort. You must show them by explaining your experience and passion to solve the problem.

- **Explain why you chose them.** Each person on your team must fully understand their role. Explain it to them. Edify them by telling why they are uniquely qualified to share the experience with you and the rest of the team.

- **Don't be entitled.** It takes time to build a strong and healthy team. You may have the best intentions, but you're dealing with humans, and they're flawed, just like you. Give them space and time to grow with you and the others on the team.

- **Identify and create boundaries with your team.** They have lives, too. Boundaries help them manage their lives in a healthy way. For instance, I don't bother my teammates "after hours." I don't bother them when they're spending time with their families. I'm not demanding of their time.

- **Manage expectations.** Expectations are dynamic, so make sure you're continually aware of them with each team member. For instance, one of my team members is having a baby soon. Her role is very important to me but not more important than her new child. We've met on several occasions to discuss how things are changing with her expanding family and how our relationship can remain mutually beneficial moving forward.

- **Be an encourager.** Remember, emotion trumps logic. So be an encourager because people will remember how you made them feel. Always look for ways to uplift your team because you can never go wrong with encouraging others.

Puzzle piece: Review the list of your top five most important relationships. Evaluate each relationship by identifying what kind of team member each person is and if they are in the right spot on your team.

Chapter 13

THE POWER OF SYSTEMS

Perfect Day Element #7: Build Systems

> *The student has goals. The master has systems to reach his goals.*
>
> —Maxime Lagacé

When I arrived at West Point in the summer of 1991, my only glimpse into the life of the military had been the chats I'd had with my father, an air force veteran, and what I saw in the movies.

I quickly learned that the army was nothing like what I expected. It wasn't action packed like I'd hoped. We spent most of our time training but not the kind of exciting training I desired. It was more monotonous.

We spent hours training on repetitive tasks. We drilled on the basics of being a soldier so much that I could do many of the tasks without thinking about it, which was the point. The army calls them battle drills. They're a set of basic skills and repetitive tasks that are necessary for survival.

War is chaotic, stressful, and exhausting. Soldiers have only so much physical, emotional, and mental energy, so the military identifies critical tasks that soldiers must learn to survive and forces them to drill on those tasks so much that they don't have to spend critical energy thinking about those tasks during battle. They can execute them robotically, which allows them space to focus on other critical tasks as the battlefield evolves around them.

There are also battle drills in life.

If you wish to not only survive life but thrive and live a life of significance, you're going to need as much mental and physical strength as possible, which is why systematizing some areas of your life is an important part of your success.

The purpose of building systems is to create space in your life so you can focus on the main things that will move the needle toward significance. This space allows you to do the things only you can do.

This is a beautiful place to be in your life.

Developing the right system that works for you and allows you the freedom to pursue significance is a lifelong pursuit. It takes time to install the necessary systems to create margin in life, so be patient and prepare for the journey.

There are five guidelines to a good system.

Guideline #1: Delegate

Don't view delegation as passing the buck to someone else. What may be a weakness for you is a strength for someone else.

To prune your recurring task list, review each task and ask yourself four questions:

1. Can others do this task just as well as or better than you?

2. Does this task drain you?

3. Does this task distract you from your purpose?

4. Is this task still relevant?

If any of your tasks meets one or all of these, then it's a candidate for delegation.

Once you decide to delegate a task, think about who within your network is strong in the task you want to delegate. You may also consider trading tasks with someone. You can offload your weak areas and take on more tasks that engage your superpower.

This is where your relationship activities pay dividends. If you've invested in key relationships within your network, then it's easier to delegate within those strong relationships.

One way to delegate is to consider hiring virtual assistants. These high achievers are willing to partner with you on specific tasks that are strengths for them. Currently, I have two virtual assistants on my team. You can search the internet for reputable recruiting services that can match you up with a virtual assistant.

I also delegate landscaping, handiwork, calendar and email management, social media, website updates, and a variety of other things.

Guideline #2: Automate

Some tasks are ripe for automation. I ask these questions with each task when considering it as a candidate for automation:

- Can this task be handled with technology?

- Can I create a template for this task?

With that in mind, I automate bill paying, robot vacuuming, email filtering, campaigns, and outdoor lighting.

Subscription services are on the rise and can be a great source for automation. There are memberships for everything from getting clothes mailed to you monthly to having someone swing by your house and detail your car.

Another way to automate is to streamline recurring tasks with predictable routines. I've found that your body is like a machine and accepts routines well. The more routines you can build into your days and weeks, the better.

Having certain days of the week designated for specific activities builds a rhythm that makes it easier for you to focus and experience increased productivity.

For example, you may choose to engage in external meetings with clients in the afternoons on Tuesdays and Thursdays. Maybe you block out Friday afternoons for weekly planning. The goal is to identify certain days or blocks of time during the week and build them into predictable themes that help you to focus.

Here's my current weekly schedule and the themes I created:

- Monday:

    * Mornings: Prepare for speaking gigs

    * Afternoons: Internal team meetings

- Tuesday/Thursday: External meetings and virtual presentations

- Wednesday:

    * Mornings: Content creation

    * Afternoons: Personal projects

- Friday:

    * Mornings: Finances and personal growth

    * Afternoons: Family time

- Saturday: Personal growth and family time

- Sunday: Reflection, church, and family time

Templates are another way to automate your brain. They allow you to translate recurring activities into repeatable activities to conserve mental energy. Use a checklist for any activity that requires the same set of tasks to be completed, such as:

- Recurring meetings

- Packing for travel

- Virtual studio startup and shutdown

- Managing personal and business finances

- Planning retreats

My mentor and coach, Michael Hyatt, taught me the value of a morning ritual when he shared his during a training session I attended. A morning routine helps to get your day started and build momentum for the rest of the day. It prepares your mind, body, and soul to take on the challenges of the day.

Building a morning routine takes time, so be patient and figure out what works best for you. For example, if you have a newborn in the house, your routine may be shortened and disrupted often because your newborn's needs come first.

Here's my current morning routine:

I wake up at 4:50 a.m. and get out of bed at 5:10 a.m. I drink a glass of water as a trigger to start my routine. Then I work out for forty-five minutes, feed the dogs, and shower. I spend thirty minutes reading, an hour writing, and thirty minutes planning my day. I do all this before 8:00 a.m. every day.

This routine takes me three hours. It's become an effective runway to launch my day and works great for me. I also use routines for weekly, quarterly, and annual retreats.

Guideline #3: Ping Critical Areas of Your Life

Like a naval submarine, you must ping your life to make sure you're not on a crash course with your own "iceberg."

I suggest you ping your life in the following areas:

Email

Send targeted group emails to your network to assess what's of value to your network. I use automated email campaigns to ping my network on various pain points. I use data from those campaigns to discern what my audience is looking for in terms of solutions, future products, and services I could develop.

Check with stakeholders

Don't allow your important relationships to become stagnant. I reach out to important relationships within my network to evaluate the strength of those relationships and look for gaps or issues with them so that I may fix them before they become damaged. I evaluate my interactions to ensure they're not overly transactional. If they are, then I try to schedule some one-on-one time to strengthen the relationships.

Personal growth

Remain diligent in your own growth. Remain relevant by feeding your mind with new material that will allow you to grow and evolve as the world evolves around you. To do this, you need a reading plan, a mentoring plan, and an education plan.

Personal retreats

Use retreats to build in pauses in your life. This is important because these pauses become mechanisms to pull you out of your daily grind and allow you to reflect and evolve with the dynamic elements of your life.

Block off one hour a week to reflect on what worked and what didn't work during the past week. Look for patterns in your behavior or the way you approach your week. Then develop methodologies to work around the necessary areas of your life.

I do a one-hour retreat every Sunday morning. I use a journal that poses a series of probing questions to stimulate my thinking. You can search the internet for a journal that works for you, but I recommend a notebook to record your thoughts and ideas.

Also, block off one to two days a quarter to reflect on the previous quarter and plan the next one. Identify the good, the bad, and the ugly of your life, and reflect on ways to elevate and enhance your journey.

When I do my quarterly retreats, I spend the first day focused on my finances and ensure that my personal and business finances are in order. I spend the second day reviewing my journal and reflecting on how I handled my challenges. I also assess my thought patterns and identify trends in my thinking and anything that might be a red flag.

I review my goals, update them, and identify what goals I plan to focus on going into the next quarter. There are plenty of planning systems on the market. Find one that works for you.

Block off at least three days or up to an entire week for an annual retreat. Use this time to relax, evaluate, plan, and reset for the upcoming year. This is a time to mourn losses, celebrate wins, and gain perspective on your life.

I build plenty of space in my week to rest and recuperate from a long year. I follow the same guidelines I use in my quarterly retreat. I just provide myself more space and time to reflect on my life and relationships.

I follow the after-action review (AAR) format that I learned when I was in the US Army. It's a solid methodology with a set of targeted questions that force you to take a deep dive into your life.

I recommend you go through these AAR questions during your quarterly and annual retreats:

- What was supposed to happen?

- What happened?

- What went well?

- What didn't go well?

- What do you need to improve?

- What do you need to eliminate?

- What do you need to start?

When planning quarterly and annual retreats, these are the best practices I follow to ensure success:

Change environment. This becomes a trigger that you're going into retreat mode. Go somewhere that stimulates your thinking and motivates you to reflect on the past and plan.

Eliminate distractions. Get rid of anything that may distract you or disrupt your process. Turn off your phone. Disable notifications on your computer, and unplug the television. Allow yourself uninterrupted thinking time so that you can get the most out of the retreat.

Take time for self-care. Preparing your mind, body, and spirit is essential to get the most out of your experience. Ensure you build in time for a full night of sleep, exercise, proper nutrition, and relaxation. It's counterproductive if you're exhausted, stressed, and feeling crummy because of a poor diet. Set yourself up for success and take care of your body going into the retreat and during the retreat.

Guideline #4: Measure Success

You naturally focus on the things you intentionally measure. Choose measurements that influence you and your team members' behavior. Most importantly, keep it simple.

Currently, I measure my exercise, rest, hydration, eating habits, weight, revenue, and cash flow. My team measures our client interviews, travel, social media usage, and finances.

Guideline #5: Record Progress

Use your key measurements to track your progress and look for trends during your quarterly and annual retreats. To achieve this, you must leverage tools to effectively record those measurements.

I record my progress in different areas of my life using customer relationship management (CRM) software, such as Evernote, spreadsheets, a paper journal, and various smartphone apps.

Building a system provides you with the space to achieve significance. Leverage the methodology I recommend, or pull from the parts that work for you and leave the ones that don't, but develop a system that gives you the opportunity to find success on your journey.

Puzzle piece: Commit to weekly and quarterly retreats. Start by picking one day a week for a weekly retreat, and carve out one hour to reflect on the previous week and plan the next one. Pick at least one day, preferably two, to commit to a quarterly retreat, and block it off on your calendar. Follow the methodology outlined in this chapter to reflect on the previous quarter and plan the next one.

PRINCIPLE 3

LEVERAGE THE POWER OF ENCOURAGEMENT

Encouraging words can be powerful and are often what we need to get us through a difficult time. Especially when we get to the point where another cup of coffee just won't cut it!

—ELLE SOMMER

PATSY, A MARRIED MOTHER OF TWO YOUNG CHILDREN FROM Indiana, desired to be a present mother to her children and caretaker of her home, but she also desired to contribute to her family financially.

That was why she joined Home Interior & Gifts in 1973. Home Interiors was a direct sales marketing company that was founded by Mary Crowley, a single mother of two, in her garage in Texas in 1953.

Patsy thrived in the business and became a director in Home Interiors by 1983. Because of Patsy's new position, Mary Crowley invited her, along with all the other new directors from across the country, to the Home Interiors headquarters in Dallas, Texas.

Mary personally trained all the new directors and spent an entire day teaching them how to be successful in their new roles. Patsy cherished this training because she was a rising star in the business and she looked up to Mary as a mentor and an example of how she should live her own life.

Mary concluded the training and released the group to head home and apply what they had learned. Patsy gathered her things and prepared to leave; however, she felt someone lightly tug on her arm. Patsy turned to find her hero, Mary Crowley, looking into her eyes. Her expression was kind but confident. She leaned toward Patsy and whispered into her ear, "Patsy, you are going to be huge in this business."

Mary politely let go of Patsy's arm and walked away from her. Mary's words of encouragement stunned Patsy and sent tingles up her spine. Mary Crowley was a big deal by that time because she was highly successful and often sought out by the political and social elite; however, she knew Patsy by name.

That was all Patsy could think about on her flight home to Indiana. When she arrived home, Patsy was determined not to let Mary Crowley down, so she gathered the top performers in her business and developed a plan to succeed.

What Mary did not know about Patsy was that she was in deep despair in her life—her own rock bottom. Patsy had found herself with significant financial issues, and she was smothered in consumer debt. To make it worse, her husband had no idea because Patsy had hidden it from him. Her marriage was on the rocks, and it was teetering toward destruction. Patsy's situation was so bad that she'd contemplated suicide.

Mary could not have known Patsy's situation, but when she whispered those words of encouragement—"Patsy, you're going to be huge in this business"—it was like she was throwing a lifeline into a raging sea of despair. Patsy desperately held on to that lifeline until she could pull herself out of her situation and claim her life back.

Mary's words of encouragement saved her life.

Mary's encouraging spirit was a cornerstone of her profound success. She encouraged women like Patsy thousands of times throughout her business career, which was how she achieved a significant life.

Patsy's story is particularly inspiring to me because she is my mother. I started this book with that pivotal conversation I had with my mother when I wanted to quit West Point. That conversation would have never occurred, and my mother would have never encouraged me if Mary hadn't encouraged her.

That's the power of encouragement. It's like wildfire that cannot be contained and must be passed on to others, which is why it's a critical principle of significance.

No one finds long-term success by themselves. You need others to survive and thrive, and others need you as well. The key to relationships is the emotional bonds you form through encouragement.

In the end, the primary thing people care about when relating with you is how you make them feel. Being an encourager is the foundation of relational and emotional success. It is my belief that the world truly belongs to the encourager.

How do you embrace and grow an encouraging spirit?

I believe you start from within and become encouraged yourself, and then you shift your focus to others.

Let's get started.

Chapter 14

LIVE YOUR STORY

Owning our story and loving ourselves through that process is the bravest thing that we will ever do.

—BRENÉ BROWN

LAUREN HILL WAS A THRIVING YOUNG WOMAN IN LAWRENCEBURG, Indiana. Like any other graduating high school senior, Lauren was excited to start her new phase of life and head off to college. However, Lauren wanted something more. She was a basketball star at her high school and wanted to play basketball at the collegiate level.

Lauren realized that dream when she was afforded the opportunity to play basketball at Mount Saint Joseph, a small college in Ohio. Not long after Lauren decided to attend Mount Saint Joseph, she was diagnosed with terminal brain cancer.

She was at a crossroads in her young life, and she had to decide how she wanted to spend her last days on earth. She couldn't control her circumstances, and she knew her days were numbered, so she decided to play basketball.

Mount Saint Joseph, in coordination with the NCAA, was able to manipulate the upcoming schedule and move up the first game of the season a few weeks to give Lauren the opportunity to participate. So in November 2014, in front of a sold-out crowd at Xavier University in Cincinnati, Ohio, and on national television, Lauren Hill stepped onto the court to realize her dream.

The crowd roared when Lauren made the first shot of the game and collectively sighed with satisfaction when she scored the last bucket of the game.

One year was all Lauren was given after she was diagnosed, and she lived the best life she could. Lauren's parents accepted the "best moment" award on Lauren's behalf at ESPN's ESPY awards after Lauren's death. Not only did Lauren inspire her local community and her teammates, but she inspired the sports nation because of one simple decision she made in spite of her circumstances.

What I learned from Lauren's story is that she chose to live out her story until she could live it no more.

Live your story.

Your story is beautiful and tragic, and it's yours. You must embrace it, and you must live it because your story, like Lauren's, will inspire and encourage others.

You encourage others when you choose to live your story, so stop fretting and start living.

The problem with life is that we are taught to live out certain stories. The first story is your high school experience. You're expected to get good grades, get a boyfriend or girlfriend, participate in extra-curricular activities, go to prom, and get ready for college.

Then it's time for you to live out the college story. Again, you're expected to get good grades, pick a major, party, be stupid, find a potential spouse, and prepare for a career.

Once your college experience concludes, it's time to become an adult and start your career. In this story, you're expected to find a job, work hard at that job, climb the ladder within your chosen career, make major purchases like a car and house that start your relationship with debt, and start a retirement savings plan.

Now that you've started your career, the next story is starting your family. It's time to marry the person you met in college and begin your family experience. You have children and raise them to live out the same series of stories your parents and society influenced you to live.

The cycle continues with the next generation.

I lived the story I thought I was meant to live, but I got lost somewhere between starting my career and starting my family.

I got in comparison mode. I tried to pursue a combination of the lives of people I admired. My time with Howie disrupted my story because he planted a seed of lifestyle design. I didn't desire a 9-to-5 office job. I wanted something different, but I wasn't sure what it was.

I became frustrated, and the Beast fed off my confusion and frustration.

I had a dream to be my own boss and create my own path, but I had no idea how to do it. My desire didn't fit the cookie-cutter story line that society had trained me to follow, and I wasn't sure how to break the cycle.

I felt I needed a plan laid out all the way to my last day on earth. I thought that was what every successful person did, but I was wrong. I didn't need a grand plan. I needed to live my story.

You too must live your story.

Embrace your reality. You have a reality that you must navigate as part of your journey. You may not like it and it may be frustrating, but you cannot ignore it. Lauren Hill didn't ask for or want cancer, but it was her reality and she embraced it.

So must you.

Embrace your strengths. Focus your energy on your superpower, and pursue a life that allows you to play within your strengths.

That's the story you are meant to live, so start living it.

Puzzle piece: Clarify your reality by listing all the obstacles in your life that may keep you from living your best life. Next to each obstacle, write down an opportunity it creates, and contemplate how your super-power can capitalize on that opportunity.

For more information on Lauren Hill's story and her foundation to fight cancer, please visit layup4lauren.org.

Chapter 15

ROCK WHAT YOU'VE GOT

I realized that God didn't give me cancer. Instead, He has given me the strength to get through this horrible disease.

—JILL CONLEY

JILL CONLEY MET THE PARTNER OF HER DREAMS IN BART. THEY married and were excited to start their new life together. But soon after they were married, Jill was diagnosed with stage III breast cancer.

Jill and Bart had to face the reality of the financial burden that comes with fighting a devasting disease like cancer. Not only did Jill have to endure treatments that drained her energy and devasted her body and spirit, but she also had to struggle with the mounting debt and the stress of potential financial ruin.

Jill had a wish.

Her wish was simple. No woman fighting to survive cancer should have to struggle with finances. She wanted to start a foundation that would raise money so that any woman fighting the disease could focus less on the finances and focus more on living, healing, and being with her family.

Jill and Bart launched a foundation called Jill's Wish.

This meant that Jill had to attend dozens of charity events. She had to put on a happy face, mingle with people, take pictures, and give speeches. She did all these activities while fighting for her life.

After a double mastectomy, sixteen rounds of chemotherapy, thirty-one rounds of radiation, breast implant surgery, and removal of a burnt left implant, Jill had had enough.

She would no longer fiddle with a breast prosthetic or try to pretend. She would face the world as who she was: a woman fighting a disease. She adopted the mantra that became a part of the Jill's Wish foundation: "Rock what you've got!"

Unfortunately, cancer finally won the battle and took Jill Conley's life seven years after her diagnosis. Bart Conley continues to honor Jill and leads the Jill's Wish foundation today with the same mantra Jill started several years ago, "Rock what you've got."

What can be learned from Jill's story?

You have physical, emotional, and mental scars that are very much a part of who you are. Those scars influence your decisions and how you view yourself, and they should not be forgotten or dismissed; however, they don't have to define you.

Don't run away from your scars. Embrace them. Rock what you've got.

Early in my career, I tried too hard to be something I was not. I tried to be an administrator, event planner, customer service guru, salesperson, manager, multilevel marketing star, white-collar "go to work every day with the same people" type of person.

I was none of those. It only exacerbated my situation.

I knew I loved being with and around people, but people had also hurt me. I had scars from past relationships that made me bitter and cynical. For instance, some of the people I felt closest to at work were the same people who spoke out against me during the internal investigation that resulted in my suspension. That hurt me and cut deep into my psyche. For a while, I lost confidence and withdrew from my network. How could I learn to interact with people without getting hurt again like that? I still wanted to be with people, but I became sarcastic and aggressive in my relationships to protect myself.

When I completed my tour in Germany and transitioned back to the United States for my next duty assignment, I discovered that I was under investigation by the Criminal Investigation Division (CID) for an alleged illegal activity regarding my paycheck that was simply not true. During the investigation, I discovered it was one of my own soldiers who had filed the complaint—someone I had trusted and counted as a friend. In the end, I was absolved of the charges, but the incident left me bitter.

Could I allow myself to get close to others, or would I always need to be guarded in my relationships? I didn't like that feeling; it's not my makeup. I desired to be open and honest in my relationships.

I had to acknowledge my scars, embrace them, learn from them, and discover how to leverage them to enhance my human connections.

I knew I loved being with people and networking. I had a passion for inspiration and wanted to motivate others. I just needed to figure out a healthier way to do it.

I started by determining what didn't work.

I'm not good in a formal supervisor role. I'm adept at influencing others but not as a manager.

I'm not good in settings where I work with the same people every day because I wear people out that way. I've got tons of energy, and I'm aggressive in nature. That works for a while but not long term with most.

I realized that I wasn't going to thrive in a static office environment.

I worked in the utility world and gained valuable experience that I wanted to explore, but I needed a change. I decided to leave my utility job and transition into a sales career, where I would sell energy efficiency software to utilities around the country.

It wasn't the job or the product I sold that mattered. I was able to stay engaged in the utility industry, and it afforded me a chance to lean more into my superpower. My new role allowed me to work with a variety of people and expand my network. I was slowly learning how to "rock what I've got." My relational scars didn't go away; however, I learned from them and found a way to work around them.

I found a sweet spot within my passion, but something was off. I leaned into my passion, but I wasn't living with purpose because something was missing.

My next step wasn't clear, and that frustrated me. I liked to write, and by that time I'd penned several short stories. I enjoyed the process, but I needed to do something meaningful with it, so I started a blog.

I didn't have a plan other than I committed to post on my blog once a week.

I didn't realize it at the time, but that commitment to write once a week would go on to provide me tremendous clarity on my path back to significance.

My blog became my workbench and an ointment to heal my relational scars.

The more I posted, the more I discovered what topics I enjoyed writing about and what my growing audience enjoyed reading. I was able to share some of my past hurts and publicly expose my scars, and I turned some of those blog posts into speaking opportunities. I discovered that people related to my stories and shared similar relational scars.

I began to find my voice.

A big part of my job in sales was to travel to several conferences a year to network with prospects and clients. I enjoyed listening to speakers at those conferences. I became intrigued by the concept of speaking and thought if I could find a way to speak at some of these conferences, I could gain some momentum for my sales job and increase my chances of winning more clients at these conferences.

I approached several event planners at these conferences, presented ideas for speaking topics, and offered to speak at breakout sessions for free. Finally, a few event planners took my offer, and I found myself speaking at some conferences.

I enjoyed the experience. In fact, I loved it and wanted to find ways to do it more!

My path became clearer now. I love people, and my strength is communication. Why not be a professional public speaker?

That's how life works. It's muddy and unclear until it's not. When you're deep in the weeds in your life, it's hard to see the bigger picture. That's why it's important to look for the clues around you that guide you back to the right path.

The moment I decided to leverage my passion for people, even though I had scars from past relationships, was the moment I chose to lead a life of significance. I embraced my scars and learned from them.

I decided to rock what I've got. How about you?

Puzzle piece: Identify your scars or past hurts. Acknowledge them as part of your story, and then list activities that would allow you to embrace some of your scars and leverage them in a positive way. For instance, maybe you experienced an unhealthy marriage that led to a messy divorce. How can you leverage that experience to create a healthier relationship with a loved one in the future?

If you would like more information on Jill Conley and her foundation, Jill's Wish, go to www.jillswish.org.

Chapter 16

JUST SHOW UP

*When it comes down to it, that's what life is all about:
showing up for the people you love, again and again, until
you can't show up anymore.*

—Rebecca Walker

"I need you to be strong."

Those were the words that my father spoke to me over the phone
late Friday afternoon on March 24, 2000.

I was a captain in the US Army and stationed at Fort Carson in
Colorado Springs. I had my bags packed, and right after work,
I planned to drive up to the mountains to spend the weekend
skiing with friends.

That never happened.

My dad called me to notify me that my sister, Kimberly Montina
McCormick, had passed away suddenly and that I needed to

come home. She was thirty-four, and I was twenty-seven. She was my best friend and often my counselor.

I was numb when I flew home to be with family and bury Kim. I had no emotion the first few days because I wasn't sure how to feel. It happened so suddenly and shocked everyone.

A few days after I arrived home, I accompanied my parents to the funeral home to see Kim. The showing of her body for the public was later that evening, and the funeral director allowed Kim's immediate family to come and say goodbye to her.

The doors slid open to reveal the room where my sister's lifeless body rested. I approached her casket and saw her body for the first time. She didn't look real. Her soul and her spirit were gone, and what was left didn't look like my sister.

A wave of emotion overcame me, and the flood of pain and regret flowed freely as the reality that Kim was gone hit me like a hot fire. All my energy and strength left my body, and my legs buckled beneath me as the weight of my body collapsed to the floor. I've never felt that level of grief before then.

It's in moments like this that life seems unbearable, and any type of normalcy seems impossible. I was in uncharted territory emotionally, but what happened next gave me hope in humanity, because people began to show up.

People from all walks of life and from different phases of Kim's and our family's life simply showed up. They came to the funeral home that night to pay their respects. The line of people waiting to console my family and see Kim was impressive. It was so long that it overflowed into the parking lot.

The average wait time for people in that line to console our family was over two hours.

My family and I greeted and hugged every single one of them. I don't remember a single word anyone said to me that night. But I do remember the faces, the expressions, and the presence of people who just showed up.

That was all that mattered to me and my family.

One special person showed up. Her dad was the mayor and had a great working relationship with my dad, the chief of police. The mayor and his wife were getting ready for the showing that evening, and their daughter was upstairs in her bedroom studying for a college final.

The mayor's wife went upstairs and asked her daughter if she wanted to accompany them to Kim's showing to pay their respects.

Her daughter declined to go because she was too busy studying for her final. However, something changed in her heart as the mayor and his wife were leaving to head to the funeral home. The mayor's daughter decided to go and hurriedly dressed and went to the funeral home.

The mayor and his family waited in the line for two hours before they greeted us in front of my sister's casket. It was the first time the mayor's daughter and I had met. Six months after we met for the first time in that funeral home, I asked the mayor's daughter, Alia, to be my wife. Nine months later, we were married.

Over two decades later, Alia and I are happily married.

Every time I get the opportunity to be a good husband to Alia and a good father to my kids, it's a chance for me to honor my sister's memory. Sometimes I pause and reflect on the journey I've had with my family, and I'm reminded that it was all made possible because one person, my wife-to-be, Alia, just showed up.

Are you showing up for others?

My parents are very supportive of me. Over the years, they've sacrificed much to show up to my events to support me; however, I always remember the one event that they failed to attend.

My freshman year in cross-country, my team qualified for the state meet. It was a big deal in my young career.

My parents had a trip that they had planned many months before the state meet. It wasn't their fault the meet fell on the same weekend. They went on their trip, and it was the right call. It was not their fault, but I remember them not being there for me. I can't remember all the times they attended everything else I ever did. They're great and supportive parents. But I just can't shake the memory of them not partaking in my very first state meet.

Once I had my own kids, I learned that my children don't need to hear me as much as feel my presence. My son Ryan won his middle school county cross-country meet, a great moment for him that I did not share. I was away on a business trip and missed it.

Ryan won the race but came up short of setting the county record by two seconds in that meet. When I asked him why he didn't set the record, he responded, "You weren't there, Dad. I needed you there."

His response bothered me, but then I remembered my parents missing my state meet and how I felt.

The next year, I worked my schedule around that county meet. Ryan won the meet again, and he shattered the meet record. I was the first to greet him at the finish line.

All three of my kids are actively involved in several activities. Whether Ashley is on the softball field, Adrian is competing in football or track, or Ryan is running in a cross-country or track meet, eventually they look up into the stands to see if Alia and I are present.

They are comforted by the fact that one of us showed up.

When I reflect on my own life and think about the people who've showed up for me, it's apparent that I needed them, and they encouraged me by their presence. I didn't need them to say anything special. I just needed them by my side.

Here's how you show up for others:

Slow down and be present. I know you're busy. We all are busy. Make your key relationships a priority, and build space in your life to be present in those relationships. Answer the phone when those people call you. Invest time being with them, and be willing to change your schedule to accommodate their needs.

Ask questions. Be curious about others. Discern what's important to them by asking good questions. Asking questions signals love and respect to others. When you take the time to get to know someone, it shows that you're ready and willing to invest in the relationship.

Listen. Talk less and listen more. Your close friends, family, and colleagues need to be heard. They have a lot on their minds, so hear them out.

In the end, the people you choose to do life with have just as many challenges as you do. Their issues, challenges, and problems mean a lot to them. When they look around to see who's sticking by them, they should see you. And when they do, it will leave a lasting impression on how they see you and how they view your relationship.

Don't try to be a hero. Just show up.

Puzzle piece: Review your list of your top five relationships. How are you showing up for those people? List ideas on how you can show up for each person.

Chapter 17

YOUR WORDS MATTER

A person's words can be life-giving water; words of true wisdom are as refreshing as a bubbling brook.

—Proverbs 18:4

I loved high school. I loved my fellow students, the activities, the sports, the culture, and the excitement and buzz around learning and planning for the future.

I also loved my teachers.

I was blessed to have many good teachers who impacted my views on life and prepared me for the future. The wisdom and words from my teachers influenced me, good or bad.

I enjoyed English, especially creative writing. Exploring a story in my head and writing it on paper excited me. I was in honors English and I struggled with many aspects of it, except creative writing. Or so I thought.

One afternoon, my English teacher said to me, "Erick, you're not a good writer."

Those words, whether she intended it or not, crushed my enthusiasm for writing. I finished the class and abandoned any thought of writing until fourteen years later, in 2005, when I penned that novel while on suspension from work.

Writing got me through that suspension. I liked how it made me feel and the way it stirred my spirit when I pulled thoughts from my head and penned them to paper. I liked the clarity I gained in my thought patterns from writing.

When I completed that novel, I didn't want to share it with anyone because the words of my English teacher crept back into my consciousness: "Erick, you're not a good writer."

The Beast wouldn't let me forget her words.

I dabbled in writing for a few years and rarely shared it with anyone. I simply wrote for myself. That changed when Ursula from the American Public Power Association (APPA) contacted me and asked if I would review a rough draft of a manuscript on a topic with which I was very familiar.

I read the manuscript during a flight and wrote tons of notes on how to improve it. I sent my notes to Ursula, and she responded with something I did not expect: "Erick, would you be willing to rewrite this book?"

The idea of working on this project intrigued me. I wanted to do it; however, I wasn't a good writer because that was what my English teacher told me. I sat on the project for a week before I responded.

I decided to do it.

A few weeks later, I entered into a formal agreement with APPA and found myself sitting in a coffee shop, staring at a blank notepad.

Had I made a mistake? What was I doing?

"You're not a writer," the Beast whispered in my head.

I wrote that book in utter fear. I knew the topic, but could I translate that knowledge and experience into a book that would add value and be accepted by my peers?

Several months later, I submitted the rough draft to APPA for review and edits. A few weeks later, I got an email from APPA. I was afraid to open it. I feared it was going to tell me how disappointed they were with the book and that they'd decided to go in another direction.

Instead, it was a polite email letting me know that they had made several notes and edited the book and asked me to review and approve the edits. When I opened the manuscript, my heart sank. It was full of changes.

Their editing staff found several grammatical errors and inconsistencies in my writing style. The book looked like a bloody crime scene. All the editorial comments were in red, and it seemed like there was nothing but red text dripping from the screen.

I walked away from it for a while to gather my thoughts and calm my soul. I sat on it for a couple of days because I didn't have the energy to face it. Finally, I gained the courage to review the edits in an objective way.

I realized something.

None of their edits altered my ideas. They were focused solely on style and grammar. My thoughts and ideas were intact, and their edits made the manuscript better.

I became encouraged.

I accepted most of the edits and resubmitted the manuscript. A few months later, the book was published. A few weeks later, I attended an APPA-sponsored conference. They had a table set up with various publications.

My new book was on the table among them.

I picked it up and held it for the first time. It was cool to the touch and felt good in my hands. I thumbed through the glossy pages and smiled as I read my own words within its pages.

In that moment, I realized that I was indeed a writer.

It wasn't that I didn't have ideas or couldn't write. I wasn't a strong editor, but I didn't need to be strong in that skill to successfully write books.

This book you're reading now is my sixth book.

It took over two decades to overcome my English teacher's statement and get the courage to write and share my thoughts with the world. I shouldn't have let her words impact me the way they did, but her words mattered to me.

Your words matter to someone as well. Are you using them for good?

Your parting words fuel how people feel about their interaction with you. Because I've experienced sustained success in my public speaking career, I've had several professionals approach me for advice on how to speak successfully. I teach them that what you say in the final moments of your talk is what people remember the most, so choose what you say wisely.

The same applies to every human interaction.

It's not just what you say but also how you say it. Your tone and delivery are just as important as what you say.

My tone hurt my marriage and my kids' early childhood because I often raised my voice. Once I raised my voice and brought an aggressive tone to the interaction, my message was no longer heard because emotion trumps logic. It wasn't until I learned to control my emotions and use my words to connect and edify my family that I truly became the husband and father my family deserved and desired.

When your words and tone spark a negative emotion, you lose the connection. Use your tone to edify and heal, not destroy.

My lack of discipline with my words is what got me suspended at work.

I didn't realize the power of my words, and I spoke to others without a filter. When the human resources director notified me I was suspended based on his investigation, I was shocked.

I was even more shocked when I heard the findings of his investigation.

He listed off several things people reported that I had said. It wasn't what I said that shocked me but how they interpreted it. One person stated that I said, "Don't make me regret that I hired you." She felt that I was threatening to fire her. When he read that statement to me, it sounded horrific. Out of context, I agreed with the woman; however, I knew my intent. I liked her and valued her. I was bantering. But it didn't matter. It was how she perceived it that mattered.

I sat in silence as the human resources director expressed his concerns for over forty-five minutes. It was hard to listen without responding, but it was the most valuable forty-five minutes of my career.

It humbled me, and I needed to hear it, learn from it, and evolve.

When I pulled up to the municipal building before meeting with my boss and the human resources director that day, I wrote a note to myself and left it on the seat of my car so I would read it when I came back from that meeting. It read, "Whatever happens in the next hour, just know that you have value to bring to the world, and you will get through it."

Those words comforted me when I came out of that meeting, but if I were to survive this moment and ultimately thrive moving forward, I needed to learn to encourage others and it had to start with my own words.

All things being equal, people gravitate to and enjoy working with people they like. People evaluate that level of enjoyment based on how you make them feel. You make people feel good by the words you choose, so choose wisely.

When in doubt, be slow to criticize and quick to edify because encouraging words are the foundation of human connection.

Who will you encourage with your words today?

Puzzle piece: Identify a strained relationship you're experiencing. Meditate on how you interact with that person. Write down any negative words or tone you used with that person. How can you alter your tone and words when interacting with that person in the future to encourage them?

Chapter 18

SACRIFICE IS THE KEY TO HUMAN CONNECTION

True love is selfless. It is prepared to sacrifice.

—SADHU VASWANI

I WAS ON MY WAY TO WORK WHEN MY PHONE RANG. ON THE other end, Alia said in a calm voice, "What are you doing?"

"Heading to work," I responded.

"No, you're not. I'm in labor."

I pulled the car around, called my boss, and drove straight to the hospital.

Finally, after nearly a month of forced bed rest at the hospital, it was time to meet my twin boys.

The birthing room was teeming with activity. Alia was scheduled to give birth naturally, so there were a lot of medical staff in attendance. Some were there to assist in the birth, and others were there to observe a natural childbirth of twins.

I stood helplessly by Alia's side as she struggled to give birth to Ryan. Alia looked up at me, tears forming in her eyes. "I don't think I can do this."

"I don't think you have a choice," I responded with a pained smile.

Just after noon, Ryan emerged squirming and screaming. I watched as the doctor massaged his little body and cleared his throat. She handed me a pair of scissors to cut the umbilical cord.

A nurse pressed hard on Alia's stomach to hold Adrian, our second son, to keep him from flipping and avoid complications in the birth.

Alia grabbed my hand, and I squeezed it lightly for comfort. Her eyes locked on mine as she began to breathe heavily and prepared for round two, the birth of Adrian.

Watching the birth of my twin sons was and still is the most amazing experience of my life. To observe the creation of life in that way is a profound experience.

To me, there is no greater sacrifice than what a mother endures for her child. It begins with inception, escalates during pregnancy, and climaxes at birth. But the sacrifice doesn't end there. It's a series of lifelong sacrifices that a mother makes for her child.

I once read that there's no greater bond than between mother and her child. I believe that, and I believe it's because of the sacrifices a mother chooses to make for her child.

I recently celebrated twenty years of marriage to my wife and Mother's Day with her. We didn't think it through when we got married on Mother's Day weekend, but now every year, I'm reminded of the sacrifice my wife made for me and my children as we celebrate our marriage and her motherhood at the same time.

Sacrifice is what binds humans together.

Whenever I ask a former athlete or military veteran what they miss most about their time on a team or their military unit, they always answer the same: the people. They miss the camaraderie of the locker room or the military barracks.

Why?

Because they sacrificed for one another, and when a person sacrifices their time, sweat, blood, and tears, they form an unbreakable bond with their teammates and fellow soldiers.

I had the opportunity to experience both forms of sacrifice when I joined the varsity cross-country squad at the United States Military Academy in 1991. We formed a bond that is just as strong today as it was back then because we experienced something special together that was unique to us.

For instance, while at West Point, I logged over 11,000 miles with my teammate Jack.

Not only did we sacrifice with each other, logging thousands of miles in the cover of darkness while others slept, but we also sacrificed for each other while on deployment protecting our country's way of life.

I was assigned to the 536th Military Police Company, known as the Gladiators, while on deployment to Bosnia-Herzegovina. I was a newly minted twenty-two-year-old second lieutenant and platoon leader of the second platoon, the Wolfpack Platoon.

I struggled in the beginning.

The good news was that I had Tim. He was a fellow platoon leader from the 615th Military Police Company.

Tim's platoon was on temporary assignment to our company. Tim and I consoled each other many times, and I found comfort in his company. We spent nearly a year in Bosnia, sacrificing for each other and strengthening our bond. I'm still connected with Tim today. We formed a bond few can understand because of the sacrifices we made for each other during our deployment to Bosnia.

When you sacrifice for another human being, that person recognizes and acknowledges your sacrifice. Your souls become connected.

There are three ways we sacrifice for one another: time, money, and ego.

Time

It's the most precious asset you have, and when you give it to someone, it's an active sacrifice for them.

Once I settled into my role as a father, I began to reflect on how I could connect with my kids. I realized that I formed a connection with my dad when I began to run with him. The time we spent running and traveling to various races on the weekends allowed my dad and I to bond and connect. Our connection grew as he traveled to various cross-country and track meets to cheer me on during middle school and high school.

I wanted that same bond with my children, so I decided to use sports to connect with them.

For Ashley, it was softball. I didn't know anything about softball, but I jumped into the sport to support my daughter. We spent countless hours on the field, in the batting cage, and traveling to weekend tournaments. Many of those hours were downtime, with us just talking and connecting with each other.

I gave Ashley my time and attention, which formed the foundation of the connection we have today.

For Ryan, it was running. I started running with my dad when I was eight years old, and Ryan began running with me at the age of nine. Our first run together was four miles on a trail known as the B-line trail in Bloomington, Indiana. It would be a trail that became a place Ryan and I would spend many hours and hundreds of miles running together and getting to know each other.

For Adrian, it was different. He wasn't particularly athletic at eight or nine years old. He became much more athletic a few years later. In the beginning, I looked for other ways to spend time with Adrian. I took him on a planning retreat in Nashville, and we spent the week dreaming about our future.

We bonded that week.

Ironically, one of Adrian's goals he crafted during our retreat was to try out ten different sports. That planted the seed for his football and track career. I also took Adrian with me to West Point to reunite with my cross-country and track teammates. The time we spent together that weekend inspired Adrian to look at West Point as a possible higher education choice.

Money

Finances are deeply personal, so when you sacrifice money for another, you solidify the bond with that person.

Our culture doesn't like to discuss finances in a social or casual setting. You just don't ask someone, "How much money did you make this month?"

For several years, I struggled financially. When I left the military, I didn't start out with a high-paying job, and I made poor financial decisions.

One year, my former West Point teammates decided to coordinate a reunion in Boulder, Colorado.

I declined to attend.

My lifelong friend and teammate Jack called me. "Hey, man, you need to come to this reunion. It won't be the same without you."

"I get it. I just can't make it," I responded.

"Is it about the money?" Jack asked.

I dropped my head in shame. I couldn't lie to my friend. "Yes," I whispered.

"Don't worry about that. I can help you. We want you with us."

I had some frequent flyer miles saved in my account with United Airlines. I needed a few thousand more points to get a ticket, so Jack transferred the necessary miles from his account to mine.

Tim, my former teammate who served with me in Bosnia, asked me to stay with him in his room and didn't ask for reimbursement.

John, the former officer in charge of our cross-country team, picked me up at the airport so I didn't have to incur expenses getting to Boulder from the airport.

Mike, another former teammate, drove me back to the airport after our reunion weekend.

I spent less than $100 that weekend and created wonderful memories with my closest friends all because of the sacrifice of money. Our bond grew stronger as a result.

Ego

When you are quick to apologize and approach another with humility, that person recognizes the sacrifice because we all know how hard it can be to admit we're wrong.

When a person asks for your forgiveness, it changes the dynamic of the relationship.

I recently experienced this sacrifice when a former friend, Brad, called me to ask for forgiveness. We forged a relationship because our daughters played softball together. Toward the end, our relationship soured, and things were said that fractured our bond, so we stopped talking and relating with each other completely.

One Sunday evening I was watching a show with Alia when my phone rang. To my surprise, Brad was on the other end.

"Do you have a moment?" he inquired.

"Sure," I responded.

"Thanks. I'm calling because I don't feel right about how we left things. I did some things to you and Ashley that I regret, so I'm calling to ask for your forgiveness."

My heart softened in that moment, and Brad and I had a lovely conversation for the next thirty minutes. I apologized to him for the part I played in the fracture.

My thoughts about Brad and our relationship changed that evening because Brad sacrificed his ego for me and the relationship. His sacrifice healed our bond.

Is there someone in your life right now who could change everything if they just said, "I'm sorry"?

More importantly, is there a strained relationship in your life right now that you could change if you just said, "I'm sorry"?

Relationships require sacrifice to survive.

The sacrifices you make with your time, money, and ego are the necessary elements that strengthen your bonds with others that last a lifetime.

How will you sacrifice for another today?

Puzzle piece: Identify a relationship that's important to you where you need to apologize for something you said or did. Gain the courage to reach out to that person to apologize. You can apologize through a written letter, by phone, or with a face-to-face interaction. Invest the time and effort to repair the relationship by sacrificing your ego.

PRINCIPLE 4

IGNITE YOUR INFLUENCE AND MANAGE CHANGE

The one thing you can count on is that nothing ever stays the same.

—Patsy Rheam

In the summer of 1991, my parents took me to the airport so I could board the plane that would take me to West Point and start a new phase of my life.

We waited at the gate together in silence.

When it came time for me to board the plane, my parents wept bitterly when they hugged me goodbye. I didn't understand their emotional goodbye that day.

Later, the gravity of what happened that day at the airport dawned on me, and I understood my parents' grief. What they understood then that I fully understand now is that life as we knew it would never be the same.

To that point, my eighteen years on earth were stable. After that, my life was the epitome of change.

I learned to accept and adapt to change to survive. I also learned that if I were going to live a life of significance and recruit the help of others, I needed to become an expert at guiding the levers of change.

In this part of your journey, I will show you how to manage change in a healthy and meaningful way that allows you to pursue your path to significance.

Chapter 19

THE TRUTH ABOUT CHANGE

All great changes are preceded by chaos.

—Anonymous

I arrived at Camp Lisa near the municipal town of Srebrenica late at night. Srebrenica was deep in the Serbian territory in Bosnia-Herzegovina and was geographically separated from the nearest United Nations allied base.

It felt isolated.

My new platoon sergeant was the first to greet me. He was a tall, lanky man with a crackle in his voice when he spoke. His helmet sat loosely on his head, tilted to the side. His chin strap was unbuckled and dangled to one side.

He didn't seem pleased to meet me and was short with his words. He showed me to my tent, which I shared with him. I got settled and prepared myself for the next day.

I met my platoon early in the morning. The platoon sergeant gathered them into the general-purpose medium tent. When I entered the tent, it was warm from the stove in the center. The space reeked of body odor, mildew, and bleach. I faced thirty-three men and women from all walks of life, of various social economic statuses, and from every region of the United States.

The tent was eerily quiet as everyone stared at me, sizing me up as their new platoon leader. I gave an awkward speech and then left the tent, terrified.

Was I good enough to lead this platoon?

My first week as the new platoon leader of the Wolfpack Platoon did not go well. We were assigned as the quick reaction force for the camp. We were activated within my first week, and I didn't perform well. My soldiers obediently followed my orders but did very little to hide their doubt in my leadership.

By the end of my first week, I was sleep deprived and so cold that I could barely feel my toes. I was exceptionally dirty as I had not showered since I arrived in the country because there was no running water at the camp.

I doubted I had the ability to lead my unit. I felt like an utter failure. West Point had taught me how to be a leader. I understood the concept, but I struggled to translate that training into practice. I was losing the confidence of my platoon and company leadership.

I felt alone.

One afternoon, I slipped away from my unit to gather my thoughts. I found a hillside with a little tree barely surviving the winter. I hiked up to that tree and looked around to make sure there was no one in sight. Then I dropped my head in shame, and the flood of emotions poured out in the form of an uncontrollable sob.

The Beast was painfully present and feeding into my desperation.

I gathered myself and found the strength to reunite with my platoon. I had to figure out a way to lead my platoon and survive this deployment. I just wasn't sure how.

My first impression of my operations sergeant did not go well either.

He was a large, strong, Samoan man with deep age lines in his face indicating a hard life. His dark eyes were sunken into his skull and could burn holes through you when you locked eyes with him.

He rarely smiled or spoke, but when he did speak, it was with authority. He verbally berated me on a few occasions. I later learned he did that on purpose to set an example for the other platoon leaders and soldiers.

He didn't bunk with anyone else and slept in a small tent on the hillside not far from the company tactical operations center. I could see the glow from a small fire near his tent each night and became intrigued by him.

I admired his confidence and the respect he garnered from the other soldiers.

One evening, I approached his tent and asked to speak with him. I was surprised he invited me in and spoke to me with kindness. He was different with me within the private confines of his tent than in front of the soldiers. His eyes were gentle, and he smiled. I didn't know he had teeth until that moment.

"What am I doing wrong?" I blurted out to him.

He seemed to search my eyes for an answer. "Listen to your soldiers," he responded in a matter-of-fact tone. "They know what they're doing and won't lead you astray."

"That's it?" I shrugged my shoulders.

"Trust in yourself. You're sharp and talented. Things will settle down, and you will find your place. Don't worry. Plus, I won't let you fail." He smiled.

I visited my operations sergeant every night after that, and we became great friends. He still berated me in front of the other soldiers, a role I learned he needed to play, but he was kind and generous with me during our nightly chats.

Over time, he was right. I did find my place. Things settled down, and I learned to adapt to my environment. I gained the trust of my soldiers and earned the respect of my peers and chain of command.

My deployment to Bosnia became a pivotal point in my life and was an invaluable learning experience. It taught me a huge lesson about life: Don't shy away from chaos; rise above it.

I learned that my mind and body have an incredible ability to adapt to any chaotic environment and that my instincts for survival are strong. I also learned that I needed others and that those relationships elevated me above the chaos.

Chaos usually comes in the form of change. The changes can be small or mighty, but it's disruptive all the same.

Change is part of the game that you must learn to understand.

When change occurs and you sense the tension in your life because of it, that's a sign you're on the right track. It's not comfortable to expand your horizons, but you can survive the transition and create a larger and healthier comfort zone.

The hard truth with change is that it requires people to change with you.

As you evolve, your relationships must evolve with you. To guide the levers of change and thrive during chaos, you will need powerful relationships. Some of your relationships won't survive change, and that's okay and a necessary part of the journey.

In the book *Influencer* by Kerry Patterson, Joseph Grenny, David Maxfield, Ron McMillan, and Al Switzler, the authors suggest that bringing others with you through changes requires that you influence their behavior, and one way to achieve that is through key measurements.

Peter Drucker said, "What gets measured gets done." He's right, but in the case of influence, the measurements of success should be based around human behavior.

It was Saturday night on a warm summer evening. The bases were loaded on the ball field, and there were two outs. My daughter, Ashley, was up to bat.

She approached the plate and tapped the bat against her cleats to knock off the dirt, a familiar ritual that had become part of her routine. She squared up to the plate and looked toward the pitcher, signaling that she was ready.

The pitcher looked like a giant in comparison to Ashley's ninety-five-pound frame. The girls in the outfield creeped toward the infield when they saw Ashley approach the plate. They figured a small girl like Ashley had no chance to hit the ball over their heads.

What they didn't know was that I had spent hours with Ashley in the batting cages preparing her for a moment like this.

When Ashley was nine years old, we chose softball as her activity. I didn't know anything about the sport. I observed the game for a few months and determined that we needed to focus on hitting. I didn't have the time to work with Ashley on every aspect of the game, so I decided that we would focus on her hitting, and the rest would work itself out. But it wasn't just her hitting ability that mattered. It was the ability to get on base that I wanted to lock in for her.

That would be the key measurement of success for Ashley.

"If you can get on base, then there will always be a place for you on a softball team," I told her.

So we practiced. I purchased the best bat I could find, and I hired hitting coaches to work on her swing. After each tournament, I didn't focus on how she fielded or ran the bases as much as I focused on her on-base percentage or how often she got on base.

Her on-base percentage, or OBP, went up each season, and as I'd hoped, she got more and more opportunities to play.

The pitcher wound up and threw her first pitch right down the middle of the strike zone. Ashley swung hard and missed.

Strike one.

I taught Ashley to always swing at the first pitch because it's usually the most hittable pitch.

Ashley swung and missed again. Strike two.

Ashley didn't panic. She'd been here many times. She took some pitches and fouled the ball off several times. She wore the pitcher down until Ashley found herself with three balls and two strikes and the bases loaded.

I sat in the dugout watching Ashley prepare for the next pitch, like I've done hundreds of times, and hoped she could find a way to make contact and get on base. My parents were in the stands, along with my wife and two sons.

Crack!

The next pitch came in hot but right down the middle. Ashley's muscle memory took over, and the hours of practice kicked in as her bat made perfect contact with the ball and sent it sailing over the outfielders and over the fence.

My heart leaped out of my chest, and I raised my hands in the air in victory. Ashley rounded the bases with a huge smile on her face as she realized she'd just hit a grand slam—her first time hitting a ball over the fence.

It was one of the best moments I've had as a parent and a moment Ashley and I often talk about today. I have that home run ball sitting on a shelf in my office, and when I look over at it, I'm reminded of that memory I shared with Ashley and the rest of the family, because we decided to focus on one key measurement of success that influenced Ashley's entire approach to the game of softball.

When engaging in any meaningful relationship, especially with relationships that may impact your path to significance, you must become comfortable with navigating change within those relationships. The best way to do that is to focus on a key measurement that influences behaviors. In Ashley's case, we focused on her on-base percentage, and it allowed her to navigate her softball journey.

What key measurements will you focus on with your most important relationships?

Remember, the measurements you choose should influence behavior. For sales, it can be the number of sales calls made before noon each day. If it involves your children, it can be the number of books read each month. Keep it simple, measurable, and positive.

Puzzle piece: Identify an area of your life that's in flux. Pick a key measurement that will influence others in that area of your life. Communicate the key measurement to the people you desire to change with you and begin tracking it.

Chapter 20

DON'T FIGHT THE MOMENTUM OF CHANGE

Sometimes thinking too much can destroy your momentum.

—Tom Watson

My boss, Cody, took me to the airport in Oklahoma City after a few crucial days together at company headquarters. Things were changing within the company, and I was at a crossroads in my career.

I had few great opportunities to move on with other companies, including a potential offer to become a CEO of a startup down in Memphis.

I was unsure of the path I wanted to take, and Cody sensed that during our time together.

We pulled up to the curb at the departure drop-off area at the airport. Cody helped me with my bags, and we shook hands to say goodbye.

"Listen, Erick, I know you've got some other opportunities you're considering," Cody said as I grabbed my suitcase from the trunk of his car.

I didn't say anything. I simply nodded in agreement.

"I know there are some competing offers on the table, and I can't match those financially, but I can offer you the flexibility to pursue public speaking."

I looked over at him, intrigued.

"You're a good speaker, and I know that's important to you. I want to encourage that and won't get in the way of those opportunities." He smiled as we shook hands again, and then we parted ways.

I pondered Cody's words the entire flight home. I recently started to speak more at conferences on behalf of the company, and I enjoyed it. Cody was present during many of those presentations, and he recognized my passion for it.

He was wise in offering that as a benefit to stay with his company because that was exactly what I did. I declined the other offers, even though I could have made more money, so I could continue to explore my passion for speaking. I was stressed during that time because I wasn't sure what path to take, but when Cody acknowledged my skill at speaking, he helped me clarify my path.

The source of my frustration was overthinking. I tried to map out every angle of every decision I made. I feared failure and saw it as a sign that I was making poor decisions.

I fought my own momentum because I tried to chase opportunities that were not well suited for me. I pursued so many dead-end paths because I observed other people I respected thriving in their lives, and I felt I needed to duplicate exactly what they did.

It worked for them but not for me.

I learned I could respect someone's life decisions and wisdom without trying to duplicate their journey. I was on my own journey and needed to embrace it.

You must do the same.

I pursued direct sales because I was lured by the lifestyle. My mom was successful at it, so I thought I could be as well.

I was wrong.

I didn't have a passion for the product, so it was an empty sell. I fought the momentum pulling me away from it because I wasn't sure what I would do next. I felt like a failure if I quit.

I remember the day I decided I was moving away from the direct sales path.

I announced to my family after church that we were going to Taco Bell. A simple move, but Alia noticed an immediate change in my mood. I'd developed a strict discipline in my day to pursue direct sales, and I'd lost my spontaneity and zest for life. As soon as I made the shift away from it, my mood and view of life changed for the positive. It had nothing to do with the direct sales industry. It wasn't my path and wasn't for me.

Although direct sales didn't work for me, I did learn a lot about prospecting and sales, and that momentum led me to a sales role for a software company and the opportunity to leave an office environment and work from home.

That move got me one step closer to the lifestyle I craved.

I adapted well to the lifestyle of working from home and traveling to conferences all over the country. I had a passion for the people and organizations I served within my new role in sales, but I didn't have a passion for the product I sold. The momentum of change was pulling me away from that sales role and from Cody.

I fought the change.

The Beast whispered within my soul, "Why rock the boat? You've got a good thing going here." Status quo is an effective tool of the Beast, and I allowed it to delay the inevitable.

Luckily, I had enough wisdom to not fight it completely. I formed a relationship with Grant, the founder of a professional speaking and training company. Grant and I agreed to a part-time partnership that would allow me to continue to work with Cody while building my own speaking business. This partnership spread me thin, but it was the next step I needed to take on my journey.

Working with Grant allowed me to tap into a much bigger network, which I craved. The experience gave me a crash course in how to operate in a lean startup business. We worked hard, wore many hats, and did what was necessary to serve the clients and continue to grow the company.

I enjoyed working with and coaching high achievers who desired to translate their success into a speaking business and career.

It was exciting and exhausting.

Things were going well, and Grant kept offering me opportunities. He eventually asked me to be on his leadership team. I was honored by his confidence in me and accepted the role.

For a time, I attempted to manage my role on Grant's leadership team as Cody's vice president of sales and as president of my own fledgling speaking business.

I struggled to find balance.

My performance for Cody declined, and I realized I needed to decide on my sales position. Before I left for a trip to company headquarters to meet with Cody and the company leadership, I counseled with several folks on my team and decided to walk away from my job. It was a big decision and something I didn't take lightly, but it was time to move on.

Before I could speak with Cody about leaving the company, he fired me.

I did not expect it, and it hurt. Because of my declining sales and lack of focus, Cody had to let me go. I respected Cody and appreciated his leadership, mentorship, and friendship. Even though I was planning to leave anyway, it was a blow to my ego. I had fought the change for too long. Cody was right in letting me go, but it still hurt. It was a lesson learned about fighting the inevitable changes in life.

It was March 19, 2019, and I was officially off the day job train for the first time since I graduated from college in 1995. No more guaranteed salary. No more health insurance, employer 401(k) match, paid vacations, and all the other benefits that come with full-time employment.

I was on my own. I was terrified and excited.

I loved my speaking business and my partnership with Grant. I learned so much from him and the other entrepreneurial-minded folks on his leadership team. However, I didn't enjoy the administrative part of it. I had no passion for it.

I'd seen this story play out before, and I needed to learn from what happened with my last six months with Cody, so I engaged in a tough but open discussion with Grant to let him know what I was feeling.

The momentum of change was pulling me away from Grant, but this time, I approached it differently. I decided to have the conversation much earlier, and as a result, we figured out a way to alter our partnership that pulled me off the leadership team but allowed me to continue to work with Grant and the rest of the team.

My new partnership with Grant relieved me of my administrative duties but allowed me to do the things I loved and leverage my superpower. It was a win-win, a perfect partnership. I love it.

I've fought the momentum of change throughout my journey and still do because of the fear of the unknown. The Beast uses this fear to slow my momentum and get me off track, but I'm getting much better at managing it by leaning into my passion and pursuing activities that leverage my superpower. I moved toward opportunities that fueled my passion and allowed me to work within my superpower more often than not, and that made it easier to accept change.

My journey to this point has not been smooth to say the least, and I still fight change and recoil at the fear of the unknown. The key is, I'm aware of it, and I have the tools to fight it now.

I've learned that change occurs with or without me, so I might as well use it to my advantage and manage it in a way that allows me to take greater control of my own path and elevates me above the chaos.

Although change is still hard for me to accept, I'm much better at managing and riding the momentum of it by following these four steps:

1. **Acknowledge your gut feeling.** Your body is adept at change, and your instincts are usually correct when it comes to change. When you begin to feel the momentum of change occurring around you, don't fight it.

2. **Seek counsel with the influencers on your team.** You've developed and fostered these critical relationships for moments like this. It's time to leverage those relationships by getting advice on the change you're experiencing and ways to navigate it.

3. **Communicate with the people who are affected by the decisions you make regarding the change.** This may be a boss, a colleague, your spouse, or a combination of these people. It's important to have a conversation with them early in the process. The longer you wait, the bigger the problem will become, and it could damage those relationships as a result.

4. **Accept the change.** Change is a part of life, and it cannot be avoided. There are seasons of life for a reason. We're not meant to be static in our journey. A life of significance requires constant movement, and this is often fueled by change. Don't try to fight the waves of change or you will be crushed. Instead, ride the change to new levels on your path to significance.

What change are you fighting? How can you fight less and manage the momentum of it in a way that increases your chances of a more positive outcome?

Puzzle piece: Identify an area in your life that is ripe for change. Follow the steps outlined in this chapter, and look for ways to navigate the change to a new phase of your life.

Chapter 21

DISASTER-PROOF YOUR LIFE

No relationship is totally without conflict.

—H. Norman Wright

I should have been fired from my utility job back in 2005.

The only reason I wasn't fired was because of my boss, Ralph, a highly respected influencer in the community. He spent decades building trust and relationship capital with the community leaders.

Fortunately for me, Ralph used that relationship capital to save my career.

He was kind, encouraging, and helpful to me during that time. He spent several hours mentoring me, comforting me, and protecting me from myself. I was young and brash and I lacked awareness.

Ralph cushioned me from the consequences of my poor decisions.

One of the reasons I survived my rock bottom is Ralph and the influence he had on me and those around me. It was a relational lesson I've never forgotten.

If you embrace a life of significance, that means that you will evolve and change as the momentum of your journey takes you to new heights. This requires you to influence others to change, and whenever there is change, there is conflict.

When conflict occurs, you'll need the help of influencers to get through it. If you want to survive the trials of life, surround yourself with influential people who will protect you when life knocks you down and renders you weakened and vulnerable.

I call this tactic the "plus one" insurance policy.

You need only one influencer in each of the major domains of your life: your career, your community, and your family.

First, identify an influencer. They're not hard to find. They're usually involved in the community, and people respect them.

Who are those folks in your life?

Second, build relationships with them. Here's how:

- **Be curious.** Ask questions and get to know what excites and motivates them. You gain a better appreciation and deepen relationships with others simply by being curious about them.

- **Add value.** As you unlock an influencer's patterns of behavior, you'll begin to understand what they value and what matters most to them, so you can add value to them in a way that strengthens and enhances the relationship.

For instance, when Ralph's wife passed away, he was alone and didn't like it. I realized companionship was a big thing for him. When he was ready, I introduced him to friends within my network who might suit his desire for companionship. We bonded during this time as I demonstrated that I understood and cared for our relationship.

My goal wasn't manipulation. I truly wanted Ralph to be happy because I understood it was very important to him. I stopped by Ralph's office each day and inquired about his life, his kids, and his desires, and we developed a trusting relationship that saved my career when I hit my rock bottom.

When conflict occurs, don't be surprised when an influencer you intentionally befriended stands with you as you go through the fire of change and helps you to the other side.

These relationships are powerful assets on your journey to significance.

Do you have an influential person within your inner circle? If not, search within your network, and identify a person who fits this role. Then build a relationship with that person.

Investing in a relationship with an influencer is investing in your future, so who will you build a relationship with moving forward?

Puzzle piece: Identify one influencer in your life, and invest time and effort in that relationship. Make a list of things you perceive are important to that influencer, and search for ways to add value to that influencer based on that list.

Chapter 22

THE SECRET BEHIND LEGACY

We must find time to stop and thank the people who make a difference in our lives.

—John F. Kennedy

My dad struggled to help me carry a piece of heavy furniture up the stairs and into my sons' bedroom. Sweat dripped off his nose, and he winced in pain going up each step.

"Dad, you don't have to help me with this." I paused to give him a break.

"No, I do need to help you with this," he responded with a huff.

"Why?" I asked.

He looked up at me. "Because my dad helped me when I needed him, and every time I help you, I honor him." Dad paused for a moment to catch his breath. "And someday, you will help one of your kids like I'm helping you now, and when you do, you will honor me."

That's how legacy works.

The secret to legacy is not if or how you're remembered but how those you influenced during your life add value to the world after you're gone. Your legacy depends on the actions of others, not the remembrance of your name. Your deeds will be forgotten, but the impact felt from those you influenced will live on long after you take your last breath.

The problem with success is that everyone wants the credit.

Change is hard for people, and when we fail to recognize people for their willingness to change and stay with us, it's hard to keep them on our team.

Have you ever worked hard for someone and didn't receive acknowledgment for your efforts? It didn't feel good, did it? I know you don't do the work purely for acknowledgment, but it's nice to get some credit for your work, right?

We yearn to be acknowledged. It's part of the human condition. We need to feel valued, which is why leading a life of significance matters so much.

If you want to build a solid team around you and motivate them to stick with you, then you must encourage them by acknowledging their value.

Here are the ways to leverage the power of acknowledgment:

- **Be aware.** Be aware of the support group you have around you. Who is on your team, and what value do they bring to the team? Becoming aware of the value of your teammates helps you appreciate them more.

- **Acknowledge them publicly and privately.** Let them know you're aware of their value. Don't keep that inside. Share it early and often. Be authentic and acknowledge others the way they want to be acknowledged. Some don't like to be called out publicly, so don't force it. A simple handwritten note is enough. It's not the way you acknowledge them as much as that you take the time to do it.

- **Don't take the credit.** Rarely do you accomplish anything of substance by yourself. Don't take the credit for your accomplishments because there's a strong chance that others helped you. I know it feels good to reap the fame and glory of a win, but others desire that as well. Don't be stingy and don't hog the victory.

Be generous with your praise and properly acknowledge those who deserve it.

Is there someone right now who needs to be acknowledged for the role they've played in your journey? What are you waiting for?

Acknowledge them today!

Puzzle piece: Identify a recent project or event that you success-fully completed. Now list the people who helped you. Look for ways to acknowledge each of them in a way that will honor them.

PRINCIPLE 5

MASTER COMMUNICATION AND HUMAN DYNAMICS

You will be judged based on how you communicate.

—MY WEST POINT ENGLISH PROFESSOR

I WAS AFRAID TO OPEN THE EMAIL. I STARED AT IT FOR A LONG time. I could feel the lump forming in my throat, and I struggled to breathe.

This could make or break my entire summer at West Point.

The email was from my English professor and would notify me if I'd passed or failed the final exam. If I passed, I could continue my West Point experience and look forward to the next phase of my journey.

If I failed, then I would have to retake the class, and I'd get one more shot to pass or be dismissed from school. It was the hardest college final I'd experienced, and it totally stressed me out.

The final seemed simple. A question was posed, and I had to answer with a handwritten long-form essay of a certain word count. I was not allowed any resources other than a pencil and blank paper.

I had four hours to complete the exercise, and the essay had to be error-free. One grammatical or spelling error resulted in failure.

West Point is a leadership institute. Its primary mission is to develop and train our nation's leaders who "serve the common defense." One major component of leadership is communication.

West Point hammered communication as a must for leadership and set high standards in all areas of the academy experience, including this English final.

Luckily, I passed that exam and eventually graduated, but that experience stuck with me and was a lesson in the importance of communication. If I wanted to lead a life of significance and have an impact on the world, then I would need to master communication.

In this last section of the book, we'll explore the principles needed to master communication and the role communication plays in human dynamics.

Chapter 23

WHAT MOTIVATES US TO DO WHAT WE DO?

We consume our tomorrows fretting about our yesterdays.

—Persius

My platoon spent hundreds of hours patrolling the cities and towns in Bosnia-Herzegovina. I spent hours observing the locals and their culture, and I became familiar with the landscape and the rhythms of the Bosnian people. What struck me was the droves of young men loitering the downtown areas of these cities.

They roamed the streets with no purpose.

These young Bosnian men caused trouble often, mainly because they were bored. They had energy and desired something better, but they had no means to achieve it.

I also learned a lot about the soldiers within my platoon. We spent a lot of time together, and I learned plenty about their families, their lives back home, and their dreams of the future.

Whenever we weren't on a mission, the platoon sergeant kept them busy with menial tasks like cleaning out their living space, cleaning weapons, and practicing battle drills.

My platoon sergeant taught me that "an idle soldier is a dangerous soldier."

Toward the end of our deployment, I sensed the restlessness of my soldiers. The Summer Olympics were going on that year, so I concocted a plan to keep them busy by creating our own Olympics. I called it the Wolfpack Olympics.

I crafted several competitions: basketball, the 100-meter dash, a Ping-Pong tournament, a foosball tournament, weightlifting, and several others. The squads competed against each other. I even recruited my father back home and asked him to get trophies and certificates made and shipped over to us.

My goal was to keep my soldiers occupied and out of trouble. It worked.

My experience with the darkness of humanity in Bosnia ignited my desire to study human dynamics. The core question I sought to answer was simple.

What drives human beings to do what they do? What motivates a person to hurt another living being? What drove an entire nation of people to destroy one another in Bosnia? What drove a nation like Germany to take on the world during World War II?

At first, I thought it was purpose. On its surface, that made sense to me. People need purpose, and a pursuit of purpose drives their decisions. However, there was something deeper and more sinister at play that I believe is at the core of every decision made by every human being.

Fear.

More important is the desire to avoid the feeling of fear.

Fear is a tool of the Beast that it uses to influence our decisions. We avoid and react to what we fear.

The Bosnian people feared the influence of other religions and the consequences those religious practices may have on their cultural norms.

The German people feared the loss of their country and identity as a people during World War II.

The soldiers in my platoon feared what was happening at home and that they would continue to miss out on major family events while they were stuck on deployment with no end in sight.

Our level of fear influences our level of stress. Our level of stress influences our paradigm or how we see the world. How we see the world influences our response to the stimulus of our world around us.

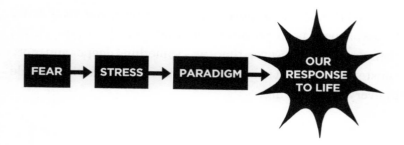

Once you begin to understand what motivates others, you don't get offended by what people do. Instead, you evaluate their actions.

Why did my spouse snap at me this morning?

Why is my top client not returning my calls?

Why did my coworker avoid eye contact with me this morning?

Once you understand that fear dominates your actions and the actions of others, you begin to understand the motivations behind others' actions.

This fundamental understanding becomes the baseline of mastering human dynamics.

My mentor, Howie, taught me that you've mastered human dynamics when people's actions no longer surprise you. Once you understand everyone is acting based on their level of fear, you begin to see patterns in their actions.

Humanity is predictable once you become aware of the fear-based response of others. You begin to see people and situations differently once you understand this concept.

Your spouse snapped at you because she's waiting to hear the results of a blood test that could have negative consequences. Her health issue has raised her stress and affected her sleep.

Your top client is not returning your calls because his business is not doing well. He fears he may need to terminate several key partnerships to keep his business from shuttering.

Your coworker didn't make eye contact with you because he had a stressful argument with his brother regarding their mother's health five minutes before your meeting with him.

Your goal is to be aware of others' fears and how they may react to the stimuli of the situation. Most of the time, a person's reaction has little to do with you and much more to do with their current level of stress caused by fear.

When you embrace fear as the factor driving most of your human interactions, you can learn to work around those issues and become a better communicator.

Puzzle piece: Write down a list of fears that dominate your thinking and how those fears may influence your responses and interactions with others. Next, choose an area of your life and the people closest to you in that area. For example, it can be coworkers, family members, or colleagues. Next to each person, identify potential fears they may have that could affect your relationship. How can you work around those fears to maintain healthy relationships? If you're not sure of their fears, then pick the most important relationship, and have a conversation with that person about their pain points and how you may be able to help them work through them.

Chapter 24

THE SECRET TO HEALTHY RELATIONSHIPS

No road is long with good company.

—Turkish Proverb

I STARED OFF BEYOND THE HORIZON, MARVELING AT THE golden sky as the sun slowly slipped into the ocean. There's nothing that truly compares to a beautiful sunset on the ocean. It stirs the soul to watch the magnificent beauty that is the transition from day into night, marked by the sunset.

On this evening, I shared the ocean sunset with Jack. We were cruising on a passenger boat on the Mediterranean Sea. We boarded the boat in Venice, Italy on our way to Athens, Greece, where we hoped to board a plane that would fly us to Cairo, Egypt.

Jack and I decided to journal while on this trip to capture our moments and reflect. We were both entering a new phase in our life as we transitioned from cadets at West Point to second lieutenants in the US Army.

We'd purchased the cheapest tickets we could get, which put us on the top deck of the boat, where we were allowed to pitch a tent with several other travelers for the overnight trip to Athens.

The temperature was a perfect eighty degrees with a light ocean wind hitting our faces. The ship gently swayed back and forth over the ocean waves. The rhythm and sound of the boat's hull crashing against the water created a methodic melody that calmed the soul and provided sort of a soundtrack as a backdrop to the beautiful setting.

Jack leaned on the deck railing a few feet away, admiring the view. We both understood that we didn't need to talk. Beauty is meant to be experienced with another, and I was glad I had Jack with me in that moment.

Once the sun disappeared and night began to dominate the sky, Jack turned to me. "You know, life comes down to relationships and memories. I'm glad we're creating these memories together, Rheamer."

I nodded in agreement, and then I followed him below deck for a hearty meal and a chance to create more memories.

I've thought about his words many times in my life when I'm at a critical juncture that requires a heavy decision. I always lean on the side of building relationships and creating memories.

The relationships you form are the keys to the kingdom of significance. Healthy and strong relationships are nurtured within comfort zones.

Society teaches us that success is on the other side of our comfort zones, and this is true when it comes to personal growth; however, it's not true for maintaining healthy relationships.

We seek comfort in our relationships. We're emotionally charged beings, and our relationships are a way for us to balance and ground ourselves emotionally so we can face the challenges of the world.

Fear is the foundation of stress, and stress forces you outside your comfort zone. There's good stress that triggers your comfort zone to grow. The army taught me that I can manage stress and adapt to a new normal by growing my comfort zone. But there's also bad stress that attacks your comfort zone.

The Beast waits for you outside of your comfort zone.

Good or bad, if a person stays outside of their comfort zone, they will eventually blow their top and succumb to the weight of the stress. It's impossible to maintain a healthy connection with someone who's living outside of their comfort zone, especially for an extended period.

Your goal is to be aware of a person's stress level and when they may be out of their comfort zone. Your primary goal when this occurs is to get that person back into their comfort zone so that you can sustain and strengthen the bond with them.

When you experience conflict with someone, evaluate the core issue by asking a critical question:

"What's wrong?"

Most of the time, the first response you get from that person is not the core problem. I don't know why this is the case; I just know it to be true.

The problem is that we often accept that first response as the issue and waste time trying to solve something that isn't the true cause of the conflict.

Instead of accepting that first answer, gain the courage to ask this follow-up question:

"Besides that, is there anything else?"

This is a magical question that gives you opportunity to incite another response and gets you closer to the core issue. When the person responds, ask the same follow-up question again:

"Besides that, is there anything else?"

Continue to ask that question over and over until finally the person responds, "No." Once that occurs, you can focus on the latest answer because that's probably the true answer. I once had to ask that follow-up question seven times before I got to the true cause of the conflict.

The question "Besides that, is there anything else?" provides you with a mechanism to get the relationship back into the comfort zone so you can reconnect with that person in a healthy way.

Be aware of your own comfort zone.

There are seasons when you experience life outside of your comfort zone. Be sensitive that you're primed to respond in a negative way that could be out of character because you're stressed. Give yourself grace. Take a pause and pull back when necessary.

Be adept at recognizing comfort zone issues, and be proactive in managing your comfort zone and the comfort zones of those around you.

Are you experiencing a conflict with someone now that could be a result of being forced outside a comfort zone? If so, reach out to that person today, and use the follow-up question methodology to begin the healing process and get back within a comfort zone where a healthy relationship awaits you.

Puzzle piece: Think about your various close relationships that might have some level of conflict. Pick one of those relationships, and reach out to the person and use the follow-up question methodology, "Besides that, is there anything else?" to work through the conflict with that person.

Chapter 25

HOW YOU SAY IT MATTERS

The sweetest music is not in the oratorio, but in the human voice when it speaks from its instant life tones of tenderness, truth, or courage.

—RALPH WALDO EMERSON

ONE NIGHT, DURING A FAMILY DINNER, MY DAUGHTER, ASHLEY, brought up an issue that apparently all my kids experienced with me that caused them stress.

"Dad, I don't like when you text me, 'Come see me,'" Ashley stated while sipping her water.

"Why is that a problem?" I asked, curious about her statement.

"Well, it always makes me feel like I'm in trouble, and I don't like it," she responded.

"Same," Adrian chimed in.

"Me, too," Ryan jumped in as well.

Alia smiled at this conversation.

"What?" I shrugged my shoulders at her.

"You do have a tone sometimes, Erick, especially with your text messages," Alia stated.

"Really? I have a tone?" I leaned back in my chair.

"Yes!" Ashley put her water down at the table and leaned toward me. "Do you have to be so cold about it?"

Since that conversation, whenever I need to speak with one of my kids, I text, "Come see me. No, you're not in trouble!"

Tone matters in conversations. Some studies suggest that the tone and inflection in your voice is 38 percent of communication.

People pick up cues and intent with how you say something even over what you say. How you say it is more important to them.

If you wish to lead a life of significance and you embrace the fact that you need others, communication will be how you connect with others. Part of that communication is tone, so being aware of your tone is critical in your relationship success.

A tip I learned early on is to smile when I speak.

It's impossible to have a negative tone while smiling. This also applies while texting. Try smiling while you text. It influences how you text someone. A warm smile softens your tone, and a soft tone is like a warm blanket on a cool, fall evening.

It's comforting.

When you interact with your inner circle, it's important to be intentional with your communication. Email should be used as a tool for information exchange only. Texting is good to fill the gaps in communication and respond quickly or to get a quick response from someone. Social media is mainly for entertainment. It's like junk food or reality TV. It rarely enhances a relationship. Don't depend on it.

People need to hear your voice.

They need to hear your tone and inflection, your accent, your cadence. It deepens and strengthens your relationships. It adds texture and layers to your relationships that electronic communication cannot.

Be aware of your tone when speaking to others because your tone will dictate the mood of a relationship and enhance the emotion of the relationship, good or bad. Don't get lazy with your communication by sending a quick text message. Pick up the phone and call that person.

If the relationship matters to you, invest the time in it and strengthen it by leveraging a positive tone and allowing people to hear your tone.

In the end, your tone will influence the emotion of others, and people will remember how you made them feel. Never underestimate the power of your tone, and use it for good.

Puzzle piece: Scan your list of your five most important relationships. Think about your last few interactions with each person. What platform did you use to engage these people? Did you engage them with email, text, social media, phone, or face-to-face conversation? Identify the interactions where you engaged in only email, text, or social media. Take a moment to call those people so you can engage with them by leveraging the tone of your voice.

Chapter 26

WHAT'S THE BODY GOT TO DO WITH IT?

The human body is the best picture of the human soul.

—LUDWIG WITTGENSTEIN

I TRIED TO MAKE OUT THE FACE OF THE COMMANDING OFFICER standing several feet away from me. We'd discovered a Serbian training camp not far from our base of operations near Srebrenica.

My base commander decided to activate our quick reaction force (QRF) to display our military strength.

I was the leader of the QRF that night.

It was my job to lead the QRF to meet my commander's intent but not to incite an international incident.

"I see movement on the ridge line!" my squad leader yelled out from a short distance behind me.

"Got it! Keep an eye on it!" I yelled back.

I could feel the tension among my soldiers and the opposing force in front of me. The commander of the enemy training camp walked out to face my team and me as we approached his unit. He was flanked by a handful of soldiers—all tense and gripping their weapons. It was the middle of the night, and I could barely make out his face.

It was up to me to de-escalate the situation.

I turned to my team of soldiers standing beside me. "Stay here and keep an eye on that ridge line. Let me know if anything changes."

"Roger that," my squad leader responded.

I motioned for our interpreter to come with me as I slowly approached the opposing commander. I made a point to sling my M16 semiautomatic rifle over my back and raise my hands with my palms facing the commander to let him know that I was not a threat.

As I approached him, I unbuckled my helmet and removed it from my head so he could see my face. It further signaled my peaceful intent because now my hands were occupied with my helmet and could no longer grab my weapon from my shoulder or the 9 mm handgun holstered on my right hip.

The commander slung his weapon over his shoulder and removed his helmet in response to my gesture. I could feel the tension melt away as we made eye contact. He wasn't much older than me, and I could see the fear in his eyes.

He didn't want trouble either. I didn't need to hear his words through an interpreter to tell me that. I could see it in his body language.

Once our intentions were clear, we were able to engage in a quick and productive conversation. I let him know we were aware of their operation and were monitoring it, and he explained it was merely a training center and that they had no malintent.

We were both satisfied with the conversation and shook hands when it was over.

Mission accomplished.

Whatever the mind is thinking will leak through the body, and I read that a human being has the capacity to display over seven million distinct nonverbal cues.

When my unit arrived back in Germany after our stint in Bosnia, I had an unusual task of investigating two adultery cases that had popped up within the battalion.

Adultery is illegal within the Uniform Code of Military Justice and strictly enforced because of the issues it causes with morale if it's allowed to persist. The US military takes the morale and mental health of its soldiers very seriously.

The last thing that a soldier should worry about while deployed and defending our country is what's going on back home with his spouse; therefore, the military swiftly addresses any accusations of adultery.

It's nearly impossible to prove adultery unless both sides confess or there's undeniable proof through pictures or video. My role wasn't to prove it but to determine if there was an inappropriate relationship and how it affected the unit.

In my first adultery case, I was certain that there was an inappropriate relationship. So I recommended that both accused soldiers be punished for their actions, which basically ensured they would not have long and thriving careers in the military.

In my second adultery case, I wasn't sure. I was certain that one party was infatuated with the other, but it was unclear if an inappropriate relationship had occurred. I recommended the soldiers be reassigned to geographically separated units within the battalion, but I did not think their careers should be negatively affected.

How did I come to my conclusions?

Body language.

I relied on their nonverbal cues to fill in the blanks for me as I attempted to discern wrongful behavior.

Assessing comfort zone was key during my interviews with the accused parties and witnesses. Since I know every human being strongly desires to be in their comfort zone, I used this to my advantage during my interviews.

Fear challenges a person's comfort zone, and I noted anytime I observed a nonverbal cue that suggested my subject was outside of his comfort zone because of my questioning.

I looked for patterns of behavior that provided me context to the situation, and it worked.

I realized that when people lie, they fear getting caught, and that fear pushes them out of their comfort zone. I asked carefully selected questions and then watched body language on top of listening. When I noticed cues that my subject was out of their comfort zone, I dug further within my line of questioning until I was satisfied I had the truth.

I looked for four primary nonverbal cues to help monitor comfort zones:

1. **Shifting away.** My subjects would physically pull away when they didn't like a question. It could be as subtle as sitting back in their seat or more obvious when they would shift their body weight away from me.

2. **Hiding their hands.** We build trust with our hands, so when a subject's hands disappeared during the interview, it could be a sign they were hiding something. They may shove their hands in their pockets, sit on their hands, or hide them under the table. All became signals of deception.

3. **Touching their face.** I noticed that my subjects needed to soothe themselves when they became uncomfortable. Sometimes they achieved this by touching their face. Whether they stroked their neck or rubbed their eyes, whenever I saw a hand to the face, I knew they were uncomfortable.

4. **Looking down.** My subjects looked down when they were unsure. Whenever I observed this, I knew the person had no confidence behind the answer they gave me.

I leverage that experience and my knowledge of comfort zone management in many facets of my life today. I've learned to master this and use it in my all my relational interactions with others.

Body language is a powerful tool. Use it to assess a person's comfort zone and stress level.

Assess your own body language as well. Is your body language making others uncomfortable? Use positive nonverbal cues to keep others comfortable during an interaction. Something as simple as smiling or keeping your hands visible will lighten the mood.

Mastering communication is important if you wish to master human dynamics and achieve significance. You don't need to be an expert, but be aware that body language matters. Awareness will enhance your ability to communicate with others in a positive way and make stronger connections as a result.

Puzzle piece: Look at your calendar and identify a crucial meeting that requires you to physically meet with someone important to you. Use the four techniques taught in this chapter to assess that person's level of comfort, and then leverage your own body language to keep the conversation and atmosphere positive during the conversation.

Chapter 27

WHAT DOES PEACE FEEL LIKE?

The pursuit, even of the best things, ought to be calm and tranquil.

—CICERO

AT FIRST, I DIDN'T TAKE THE COVID-19 GLOBAL PANDEMIC seriously. How bad could it be? Surely, it wouldn't last that long, right? I figured it would all blow over quickly.

It didn't.

I knew we were in trouble when the NBA suspended its season and I read that Tom Hanks had contracted the virus. If the NBA was shutting down, and the guy who played Mister Rogers was sick, then this must be real!

It was March 2020, and the pandemic was in full swing. Each day, the news got worse. Depending on what news channel I watched, it was either a hoax or the apocalypse. Either way, it could have devasting effects on my business and my family's way of life.

I started to get nervous.

It was spring break, and we were scheduled to head to Tampa, Florida, to stay with Alia's parents and visit Disney World. We decided to make the trip because it was a welcome distraction from the growing stress caused by the pandemic.

When we arrived in Tampa and settled in, we discovered that Disney World had shut down, so we were forced to vacation in place at Alia's parents' house. It didn't take long for the emails to start filling my inbox. They were from event planners regarding their live events that I'd scheduled throughout 2020, and the news wasn't good. My clients notified me that they were either canceling or postponing their events.

The emails just kept coming to the point I dreaded opening them.

Going into 2020, I was excited because I was on track for a record-breaking year in my speaking business. Now that seemed all but gone as nearly $200,000 of revenue was impacted in the span of one week while on vacation in Tampa.

I became alarmed by the rate of which I was losing revenue. Could I survive this? How long could I go like this? At first, I didn't let on with my family. They were enjoying their spring break. I woke up each morning wondering what I could do to stop the pending doom.

I had no clue what to do.

One afternoon, Alia's parents rented a boat, and we headed out to Beer Can Island, an eleven-acre private island just two miles offshore from Tampa.

It was a beautiful day, and the scenery was breathtaking. We moored the boat on a secluded part of the island and spent the afternoon exploring and playing with the dogs. At one point, I sat under a palm tree, tuned into my Bob Marley playlist on my phone, and nibbled on my lunch.

I soaked in the moment and watched my family play in the clear blue waters, wondering if this was the calm before the storm and how devasting this pandemic could be for our family and our country.

The Beast got louder in my head with each waking moment. "You're going to lose everything. Your business will not survive, and you will have to find a job. Nobody will want to hire you. You'll be homeless by the time this all over."

A lot was unsure in that moment. At least I was in a beautiful place and creating memories, which was all I could control. Then my phone rang, and I decided to answer it.

"Erick, my name is Mike. I just took over the training events at NWPPA, and I heard you've done some work for us in the past," the unfamiliar voice introduced himself.

"Yes, Mike. I've enjoyed working with NWPPA for several years now. What can I do for you?" I responded.

"Well, I met with our team. We're trying to figure out some short-term virtual training solutions to help our members navigate this pandemic, and your name came up several times. Do you have anything that might be relevant right now?" Mike inquired.

"Yes, Mike. I think I can help," I responded, not sure if I had anything that would help.

"Great! What do you have?" he asked.

"Well, let me think on it for a bit. I can send you some proposals, and we can schedule a meeting to discuss some options. Sound good?"

"That sounds great, Erick. Thanks! I look forward to seeing what you have. We'll talk soon," Mike responded in a cheerful tone.

I hung up the phone and took a deep breath.

Later that evening, I cracked open my laptop and crafted proposals for two one-hour webinars on topics I thought would be relevant. I sent Mike an email with the proposals and some time slots when I would be open for a quick follow-up call.

The next day, I tapped into my team. I expressed my concern about my business to Alia first. She comforted me with her confidence.

"You're an excellent speaker, and people value your message. We're going to be fine."

Alia's words soothed my spirit. I needed to hear that from her.

I counseled with my friend and mentor, Grant. I drew comfort from my business coach, Michael, and I checked in with Jack on several occasions. They kept me calm and focused.

Later, Mike from NWPPA agreed to hire me on both the proposals I sent him. I was onto something. I sent the proposals to several other event planners within my network, and they hired me as well. I was under contract to write a book for a client, and I worked feverishly during the twenty-hour drive to and from Tampa over spring break.

I finished it by the time we arrived back home.

I also reflected on my life and business during that trip to Tampa. I realized I couldn't control the pandemic and its effects on my business and life. So I focused on what I could control.

I decided that I would lean into my passion and purpose, and I decided to invest in a virtual studio. I tapped into my network to pitch the idea of a virtual event on how to survive chaos with the very methodology that was helping me survive right now.

My network responded, and I booked several virtual events through the rest of 2020 and into 2021.

I found my groove and got my momentum back.

I didn't overthink it. I just put my head down and began to grind. I stopped watching the news and simply worked within my passion and superpower. I continued to tame the Beast.

I met with my accountant later in the year to discuss my financial situation. Both of us thought we would discuss ways to cut my expenses and adjust my financial outlook based on the effects of the pandemic, but that's not what happened.

"Do you have any expenses that you can incur now?" my accountant, Todd, asked.

"Why?" I responded.

"Well, I can't believe I'm saying this, but you need to spend money. In fact, it would be helpful if you could defer any invoices you need to send out now until 2021 to keep your revenue down," Todd announced.

My heart leaped out of my chest. I'd been working hard on my business since spring break and hadn't come up for air until my meeting with Todd. I had no idea how I was doing financially. I didn't have time to think about it.

When I looked at the numbers with Todd that afternoon, we discovered that not only had I recovered the $200,000 I lost, but I was on track to beat the projected revenue goal that I'd set before the pandemic.

I was crushing it and didn't even know it!

I sighed with relief and allowed myself to slow down and enjoy the fact that my business was more than healthy, and my family was in good shape. I decided to go on a weeklong retreat deep into the woods in January 2021 to reflect on the year and plan.

I spent hours deep in thought, hiking alone and sipping wine by a roaring fire in the lodge at night. I took time to read through my journal and evaluate what worked and what didn't, and how I could improve on my daily activities to maintain my momentum going into the next year.

Toward the end of my retreat, I felt an overwhelming sense of peace deep within my soul, and it felt deliciously wonderful. I spent so long in my early adulthood frustrated and unsettled that I wasn't sure peace was even unattainable for me. However, as I sat alone in the lodge by the roaring fire, reflecting on my life, I realized that I had never been more at peace than I was in that moment.

Why?

Because I leveraged the methodology that I've shared with you in this book. I stayed true to myself by working with my passions and leveraging my superpower. I took care of myself physically and mentally throughout the pandemic. Most importantly, I surrounded myself with high-quality people who supported me, counseled me, encouraged me, and held me accountable.

I discovered that the Beast was no longer a main character in my story and was locked away where it could no longer influence my life.

I soared high above the chaos, and I felt true peace that can only be experienced through significance.

My life is not without challenges, obstacles, and struggles, but now I'm equipped to cut through the whirlwind of it all and not only achieve significance for myself but pass it on to my kids.

And I can pass it on to you, which is why I wrote this book.

My purpose is greater than what it provides for my family and me. It's much bigger than my life. My purpose is to help as many people as I can achieve the level of peace that I feel right now.

I want you to excel in your life and be at peace as well, which is why I'm committed to staying on the journey with you.

Are you willing to join me?

Puzzle piece: Take a moment and evaluate your level of peace right now. If you were to rate your level of peace using a scale between 1 and 10, where would you rate? What must be true for you to elevate your level of peace? What's the primary pain point in your life?

CONCLUSION

WHY AM I AT PEACE?

I know my why, and I'm no longer afraid to act. Fear no longer dominates my life, and I've insulated myself from the Beast by leveraging the seven elements of the perfect day.

I strive to encourage others, and I embrace change by staying ahead of it and guiding the levers of change within myself and with those I've chosen to spend my life with.

I'm committed to communicate by understanding and mastering human dynamics. I'm aware of my tone and how it affects others. I manage my comfort zone, and I'm hyper-aware when someone I'm interacting with is not in their comfort zone. When that occurs, I make it a priority to help that person feel comfortable so I can connect with them.

I do everything I've shared with you in this book on a consistent basis. It's made all the difference in my life, and it will in yours, too.

You have a choice.

Continue down your current path. Remain frustrated with your lot in life that's dominated by fear, lacks purpose and hope, and because your life is controlled by the Beast.

Or reclaim your life. Gain clarity on your why.

You'll rediscover your passion and redefine your purpose. Most importantly, you'll gain the courage to act. By doing this, you will be equipped with the tools and the methodology to cut through the whirlwind, rise above chaos, and tame the Beast.

As a result, peace will be waiting for you.

I can't wait for you to join me.

Every journey begins with the courage to take the first step. Take yours today and begin your journey back to significance.

Start your journey by taking the Discover Your Significance Self-Assessment at www.yoursignificanceassessment.com. This is a free assessment that will give you a snapshot of where you are on your significance journey, along with some action steps to move forward.

ACKNOWLEDGMENTS

If you ever see a turtle on the top of a fence post, you know he didn't get there by himself.

—Dr. John C. Maxwell

My premise is that everyone desires to lead a life of significance and to know that their life matters. However, no one can achieve any level of significance without the help of others, including me.

I think it's critical to acknowledge the people who support us along the way. Here are my greatest supporters:

Alia Rheam. Every day, Alia chooses to be my wife and to support me, even though I've fallen short of her expectations many times in our marriage. She chooses to show up by my side and is truly the rock who keeps me stable and grounded so that I may face the Beast. She's an incredible mother and outstanding partner in life. I truly could not excel in life without her.

Ashley, Ryan, and Adrian Rheam. My legacy is invested in the future of the Rheam family. My kids continually amaze me and are the joy of my life. Their future is bright, and it's my honor to be their father.

Grandma Rheam. Every afternoon, she picked me up at school and drove me to a local restaurant, where we enjoyed a meal and discussed life. She was just shy of five feet, and it was funny to watch her drive up the street with her head barely peeking above the steering wheel, but she did it with a smile and grace.

Ron and Patsy Rheam. When I moved out of the house and relocated multiple times around the country and overseas in Europe, my parents always showed up to help me set up my new living situation. They always left my home better than it was before they visited. In every phase of my life, my parents never failed to show up and support me along the way.

Kimberly McCormick. When my sister passed away, we found a prayer journal that she had kept. We were amazed by how often she had journaled about each of us and prayed over us. Kim often called me on the phone to encourage me and tell me how proud she was of me. I miss that.

Coach Garry Courter. He coached me in high school. I struggled in senior year cross-country season, and I barely qualified for the state meet. I needed to do well in that meet to secure my spot on the team at the United States Military Academy going into the following year. The week of state, coach came to school and sat with me every day at lunch. We didn't talk much; he just sat and ate with me. It gave me comfort and calmed me down going into the final race of my high school cross-country career. I finished third in that meet, and several weeks later, the assistant coach at West Point called to offer me a spot on the team.

Coaches Ron Bazil and Jack Warner. They took a chance on me and invited me to participate in a great distance running program at West Point. The opportunity to compete at West Point altered my trajectory, and I'm forever grateful.

Jack Swift. A few weeks after my sister died, I had to move out of my apartment in Colorado Springs. Jack showed up to help me move. It was just me and him and a lot of heavy furniture. I was sad and mourning the loss of Kim. Jack showed up and did whatever was needed to get the move completed. When I thanked him, he simply replied, "We've been through a lot together. I will always be here for you." His presence that day comforted me, and he's been a positive presence throughout my life.

Steve and Cathy Rex, Howie Danzik, Theresa Danzik, Michael Hyatt, and Grant Baldwin. I needed strong mentors to help strengthen and solidify my business acumen. These men and women were instrumental in my business and family growth.

Pastors Edward Dorsey, Walt Weaver, Tim Woodcock, David Woodcock, David Norris, and Kim Norris. My spiritual growth and my journey with God is the most important aspect of my life. I have been blessed by the leadership and support from these powerful men of God.

Curt and Anne Buehler. This couple stepped in to support and nurture my marriage with Alia during an inflection point in our marriage. Their guidance saved me from my destructive patterns. I'm forever blessed by the powerful six weeks they mentored Alia and me.

Carl Erskine. He was an elder at my church where I grew up in Anderson, Indiana. He was quiet and gentle but ever present. When I went off to college, he never failed to write me letters of encouragement. When I shipped off to Germany and then to Bosnia, he never stopped writing and encouraging me. I still have a box full of his letters tucked away that I can sift through from time to time to continue to draw encouragement from his words.

Mike Bernstein, Tim Grein, Jason Stewart, and Jeff Harris. My West Point teammates and brothers have never left my side and have allowed me to be myself with no judgment. Their unconditional love and support are inspiring to me.

Colonel Johns, Captain Stuhn, Ralph Mullinix, and Cody Graves. My bosses in my career stood in the gap when I needed them the most. Their mentorship and friendship made a huge difference in my career.

Mark and Dori Lawler. I cherish their support and love for my family and their unconditional support as grandparents to my kids.

Team Rheam Productions Crew. I couldn't execute my vision or live within my strengths without my team members. They effectively manage the day-to-day operations, which allows me to lean into my superpower and live my purpose.

Rod Morrison, Todd Carpenter, and Sussi Oxenboell. I don't have the skillset to manage my finances and wealth. These folks are patient, kind, and gracious with their time and knowledge and helped me manage my finances as my business grew. They established a plan to grow my wealth that will live far beyond my lifetime. The financial future of my family is secure because of them.

Scribe Media Team. My book is better because they leveraged their strengths to help me get this book through the all the various hurdles along the way. I'm grateful for each person at Scribe for the part they played in helping me turn this dream into reality.

Public Power Industry Colleagues. There are just too many to list. I entered this industry in 2001. I knew nothing about the utility business; however, my coworkers embraced me and edified me throughout my career. Much of my speaking business success is elevated by the men and women of this industry.

My Lord. Finally, my life is nothing without my Lord and Savior, Jesus Christ. Without Him, all of it would be meaningless. As I look back on my life, I can clearly see God's hand guiding my every step, and for that, I'm forever grateful.

CPSIA information can be obtained
at www.ICGtesting.com
Printed in the USA
LVHW032012270222
712155LV00001B/92